YOUR TOWNS & CITIES IN

ESSEX

AT WAR 1939-45

To Paul

Hopefully it will bring
back some good memories!
Happy Christmas 2017

Steve + Ursula.

YOUR TOWNS & CITIES IN WORLD WAR TWO

ESSEX

AT WAR 1939-45

FRANCES CLAMP

Pen & Sword
MILITARY

First published in Great Britain in 2017 by
PEN & SWORD MILITARY
an imprint of
Pen and Sword Books Ltd
47 Church Street
Barnsley
South Yorkshire S70 2AS

ISBN 978 1 47386 041 4

Printed and bound in England
by CPI Group (UK) Ltd, Croydon, CR0 4YY

Typeset in Times New Roman by Chic Graphics

Pen & Sword Books Ltd incorporates the imprints of
Pen & Sword Archaeology, Atlas, Aviation, Battleground, Discovery,
Family History, History, Maritime, Military, Naval, Politics, Railways,
Select, Social History, Transport, True Crime, Claymore Press,
Frontline Books, Leo Cooper, Praetorian Press, Remember When,
Seaforth Publishing and Wharncliffe.

For a complete list of Pen and Sword titles please contact
Pen and Sword Books Limited
47 Church Street, Barnsley, South Yorkshire, S70 2AS, England
E-mail: enquiries@pen-and-sword.co.uk
Website: www.pen-and-sword.co.uk

Contents

The Last Days of Peace

The 'War To End All Wars' was over. It was 1918. The Armistice had been duly signed and the precious peace for which so many had fought and died had arrived. It was time to pick up the pieces and look to a happier future. Yet even in those very early days the seeds of discontent and disillusionment had already been sown.

In the spring of 1918 Spanish Flu was first reported. October saw the earliest cases in Essex and by the middle of the month it was rapidly spreading. Southend alone reported several hundred cases and Witham claimed that 200 children were ill at home. However, by December the worst of the crisis seemed to be over. Reports from early in 1919 showed that the number of new patients had dropped considerably.

As the 1920s dawned the future was viewed with renewed optimism, especially in the county's seaside towns. Tourism had been badly hit during the war years and towns like Southend-on-Sea and Clacton began to welcome visitors once more. Hotels that had been used as hospitals during the Great War could once again open their doors to the paying public. The population of Harwich, in the north-east corner of Essex, had declined during the war, many residents having relocated to Dovercourt, yet there was hope. It was believed that, being comparatively close to the Continent, life would soon improve with visitors again able to come from France and beyond. This was not to be. Towards the end of the decade the Depression struck. 1929 saw the great Wall Street Crash and this was to have international implications.

The north of England, the Midlands and Wales were all hit by a decline in heavy industry. This problem did not affect Essex so much, as the county relied mainly on light industry and agriculture, but as exports dropped, farmers suffered serious losses. Agricultural market prices tumbled internationally. Grain production had always been important in the area. In 1930 falling prices led to a deep depression in

Summer 1939 – a final holiday before the war closed many beaches. (F. J. Clamp)

the markets of Chelmsford, Colchester and Braintree. Farms came up for sale at an alarming rate and those who struggled to carry on were often forced to put previously productive fields down to grass. Unemployed farm workers were not eligible for dole money because they did not pay National Insurance. It was only when the threat of a new war grew ever closer that, with imports of food declining, there was some improvement in the farming industry.

As Essex faced problems, concerns for the safety of the country were also growing. From the moment of the signing of the Treaty of Versailles there had been concerns for the future. There were four main points in the treaty that caused major worries. The War Guilt Clause insisted that Germany should bear the blame for starting the Great War. Perhaps one of the most difficult matters was that concerning the reparations Germany was to pay for damage caused by the war. This amounted to £6,600 million, an almost impossible sum for a country that had also been devastated by the war. The disarmament clause allowed Germany only a very small army and six warships. Tanks and submarines were banned and there was to be no air force. It was also decided that the Rhineland should be demilitarized. The final term that the Germans resented was that some of their territory would be transferred to other countries. Anschluss or union with Austria was also forbidden.

It was at this time that a new and charismatic German leader emerged on the scene. Adolf Hitler hated the terms of the Versailles Treaty and he was appointed Chancellor in January 1933. Almost at once he started building up the army and weaponry. By 1935 warships were under construction, the Luftwaffe was once more in existence and conscription was reintroduced. Both Britain and France were aware of what was happening, but the main concern at that time was the spread of Communism. A stronger Germany might help to prevent this from reaching the West. Even when German troops entered the Rhineland in 1936 the two allies did nothing. The last thing they wanted was to start another war.

By this time Hitler's influence was growing ever stronger. It was in November 1936 that Germany and Italy announced a Rome-Berlin agreement. Later in the month the Anti-Comintern Pact was signed by Nazi Germany and Japan. This was directed against the Soviet Union, and later on 27 September 1940 Japan, Germany and Italy all signed the Tripartite Pact which became known as the Axis Alliance. The three countries all had expansionist plans, Germany in Europe, Italy around the Mediterranean and Japan in East Asia and the Pacific.

In 1938 Hitler was taking back land that had been removed from German control by the Treaty of Versailles. Also in that year his troops

A pre-war milliner's shop in Southend. (With thanks to Brenda Sowerby)

A reconstruction at The Essex Regiment Museum showing the swastika. (With thanks to the museum)

marched into Austria. The German leader then promised that this was the end of his expansionist plans, but within six months he demanded that the Sudetenland in Czechoslovakia be handed to Germany. Finally the British Prime Minister, Neville Chamberlain, appeared take the threat of Hitler's expansionism seriously. In September 1938 he met the German Chancellor in the hope that they could reach an agreement that would prevent war. The Munich Agreement was drawn up, giving Germany the right to have the Sudetenland region of Czechoslovakia, but the rest of that country must not be invaded. In fact no Czechoslovak representatives were invited to the discussions. One of the best-known photographs of that time was of Chamberlain returning to Britain, waving the document triumphantly and declaring that there would be 'peace in our time'.

All too soon Chamberlain's trust in Hitler was shown to be misplaced. In March 1939 Czechoslovakia was invaded. An appeal was made to Britain and France for help, but none came. Leaders of both countries still believed that war could be avoided, but they did promise to take military action if Poland was attacked, believing that this would stop the German leader from taking further aggressive action. They were wrong. On 1 September 1939 Poland was invaded and war was now inevitable. On 3 September Neville Chamberlain broadcast to the nation the fact that Britain was now at war.

CHAPTER ONE

1939
War

At the beginning of 1939 politicians were still hoping for a diplomatic solution to the growing crisis situation in Europe. However, others, especially military leaders, realized that serious preparations must be made as, to them, war seemed inevitable. By the start of January plans were announced for a huge reorganization to boost firepower. Later in January the RAF acknowledged that it was taking delivery of 400 aircraft each month. This still fell short of the German total which amounted to 600 per month. The RAF by that time had 5,800 pilots, but many more were needed. A request was made to employers to release reserve and volunteer pilots for six-month periods to allow for full-time training.

Although many former Great War airfields had reverted to farmland or simply been allowed to fall into disuse, Essex still had a number of potential airfields. Much of the land was flat and could be adapted for use as landing strips. Some, like RAF Hornchurch, were important because of their proximity to London. At the start of 1915 Sutton's Farm at Hornchurch was a tranquil agricultural area. This did not last for long. It became the birthplace of the Royal Flying Corps and a fighter airfield. In fact by the autumn of 1916 it was the base from which planes took off to help to combat the German airship menace. With the end of the Great War many of the planes were consigned to scrapheaps and the former servicemen returned once more to civilian life. The airfield was no longer needed and Sutton's Farm reverted once more to its agricultural activities. With the wisdom of hindsight it is easy to see that this was unwise, but following the Armistice most people felt that it was no longer necessary to be ready for future conflict.

An overgrown pillbox. (F.J. Clamp)

This sense of euphoria did not last for long. As early as mid-1923 compulsory purchase powers were enforced to buy 120 acres of the farmland for a new airfield. Rebuilding started and Sutton's Farm once again became home to an active airfield and one that was to play a vital role in the defence of London and the whole country in the Second World War. Later its name was changed to RAF Hornchurch. This was to be a fighter airfield, as was nearby North Weald. New buildings were erected. Although war had not yet been declared preparations were certainly well in hand.

It was also early in 1939 that news broke that the atom had been split. The process was first discovered by a German physicist, Otto Hahn, and was reported by his former colleague, Lise Meitner, who was living as a refugee in Sweden. The power thus unleashed was to have devastating effects at the end of the war.

By early February 1939 the government decided to appoint twelve Civil Defence Commissioners in case war should come. Dreams of a peaceful solution to Hitler's expansionist policies were obviously fading and on 14 February Germany launched the 35,000-ton battleship *Bismarck*. February 1939 also saw an announcement by the Home Office that there were plans to provide shelters to homes in districts, especially in London, that were vulnerable to air raids. Other potential 'at risk' cities were also to be included. They became known as Anderson shelters, named after Sir John Anderson, Lord Privy Seal at the time and the minister responsible for air-raid precautions. The shelters were steel tunnel-shaped structures that could be stored until an emergency seemed inevitable. The idea was that they should be partly sunk in the ground. The standard size was 6ft 6in by 4ft 6in, but they could be extended for larger families. They were found to be very robust and a number were converted into garden sheds once the war had ended. Anderson shelters became popular in Essex, and during the war many families made nightly journeys into the garden to sleep on bunks below ground. Earth was usually piled over the barrel-shaped roof, often giving off a strong smell and they were frequently unhealthily damp. A number of older people must have suffered badly from the effects of regularly sleeping in such an environment. In fact there were those who were very reluctant to use the shelters because of the damp. They preferred to remain indoors and shelter under sturdy tables.

Alan Parrish lived in Barking, close to London, and recalls that his family already had an Anderson shelter in the garden before the declaration of war. Gas masks too were issued early on as there was a fear that the enemy might again use chemical weapons, as they had during the Great War, with disastrous results. Alan's family shelter had two single bunk beds and just enough space between them for a person to walk on the compacted earth floor. Inside it was dark and dank and home to a wide variety of spiders and insects. As far as he can remember the family only used the shelter once.

Not every family had a shelter by the time war was declared. Houses with cellars often used these. As we have seen, even if they had outdoor Anderson shelters many people preferred to stay indoors, especially in winter. A family from Great Stamford, near Saffron Walden, sometimes visited their neighbours' cellar during raids. As the owner was an undertaker he had lined the walls with coffin lids, a rather strange and frightening addition to the décor. A cupboard under the stairs was also

An artist's impression of an Anderson shelter. (F.J. Clamp)

thought to be a safe place to shelter. In bombed-out houses it was frequently possible to see this cupboard still standing. One Southend family recalled sheltering under the stairs. There were three children, a mother and grandmother, so the confined area quickly felt very overcrowded, especially before all the usual cleaning utensils had been cleared out.

The Borough Engineer's Department of Southend-on Sea decided that written advice was needed for those acquiring Anderson shelters. This stated that the shelters were designed to provide protection against blast, splinters and debris. They should be surrounded by earth on the top, at the sides and back and on either side of the front entrance. Even the thickness of the earth needed was given – no less than 15in over the arched section and 30in at the sides, front and back. The earth needed to be well compacted. It was suggested that 30in at the sides would be best achieved by sloping it down to the ground. A small wall could be built to support the slope. The entrance to the shelter was obviously a vulnerable point and needed protection. If it was erected within 15ft of a substantial building then no further protection should be needed. If not, then a blast wall should be built in front of the entrance, possibly of earth, sandbags or brick, thus protecting those inside from the direct effect of blast. Finally, if the front did become blocked, it was advised that the escape exit at the back of the shelter could be opened. This involved turning down the two clips holding the upper portion of the middle sheet in place. It could then be pulled into the shelter and any earth piled against the back wall could be removed from inside. A suitable tool needed to be kept handy to complete this operation.

The inevitability of war was becoming ever more evident. As March progressed the British Ambassador was recalled from Berlin and Chamberlain announced plans to double the size of the Territorial Army. In Essex the Territorial Army was used in two ways. The largest of these groups, forming 65 per cent of the entire force by 1939, was available to reinforce the British Expeditionary Force (BEF) either when it was away on overseas missions or taking over its home duties. The smaller but equally important group was required for the Coastal Artillery. Essex is the county with the longest coastline in England and protection was vital in case of invasion. The government also ordered the building of more factories for the supply of weapons and there were

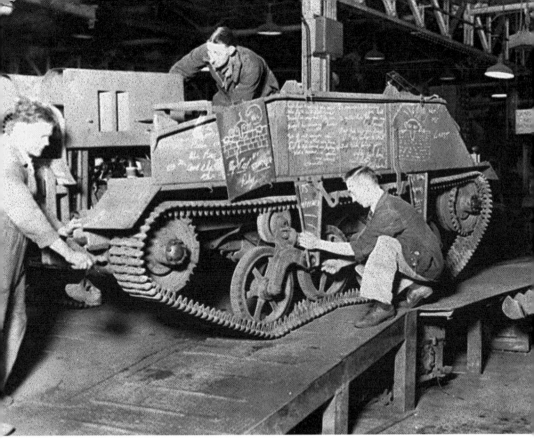

Armoured vehicles at Fords' of Dagenham. (With thanks to The Ford Motor Company)

to be extra camps and huge supplies of uniforms, including boots. More drill halls were also demanded as quickly as possible. Great Dunmow, Prittlewell and Halstead already had such buildings and soon more were commissioned in West Ham, Dagenham, Ilford, Woodford Green, Romford, Brentwood and Chipping Ongar, although not all were built.

On 31 March the Prime Minister made a solemn pledge in the House of Commons that the country would defend Poland should it be attacked. The Secretary for War, Leslie Hore-Belisha, stated that the army already had a field force of nineteen divisions and if war came the British response would not be half-hearted.

Early in April a government announcement told of plans for the evacuation of 2,500,000 children if war should come. It was realized that such a move would be a colossal undertaking. Those deciding to arrange for their own evacuation must observe the rule of women and children first. Others should remain at work. Air-raid shelters continued to be delivered and 80,000 more became available weekly. By the end of the month the House of Commons agreed to a government proposal to conscript young men of 20 years of age for military service. There were some dissenting voices and, although the Prime Minister admitted that this was 'a departure from our cherished traditions', the move was agreed. Conscripts were to undergo six months of intensive training. After that they would be transferred to either the Territorials or the Special Reserve. The Military Training (Conscription) Bill was introduced on 1 May 1939 and received Royal Assent on 26 May.

Essex farmers had faced many hardships during the Depression years. By early May, however, the tide had turned. Those working in agriculture were urged by the government to plough up their grazing land so that the amount of home-produced food could be increased. It was realized that war would mean a possible risk to any food imported from overseas. At that time less than one-third of the nation's needs was being produced at home. The farmers were promised £2 for each acre ploughed. During the Great War many people had turned their gardens into vegetable plots. This was to become ever more popular as the years of conflict progressed. Although much of this land had returned to recreational use after the war, the idea of growing your own vegetables appealed to many and today amateur gardeners still value the produce they grow themselves.

As long as war was not officially declared, some believed that peace could still be negotiated. Then, on 1 September 1939 everything changed. Shortly after 6 am, and following heavy bombardment from the air, German forces moved into Poland. On 3 September Britain and France both declared war. The days of peace had ended. The late Bernard Riley remembered clearly the day war was declared. It was Sunday morning and he was in St Mary's Church, Prittlewell for the service. It was known that an announcement was to be made at 10 am by the Prime Minister. The vicar, Canon Ellis Gowing, had asked Bernard to bring his wireless with him and stay in the vestry to listen to the broadcast. 'This country is at war with Germany', came the stark announcement. Bernard had been told to return to the church to tell the vicar as soon as he heard the news. The service was then stopped and the congregation informed. On the same day, at 12 noon, the siren sounded for the first time. Although nothing happened on that occasion it was still a frightening experience.

Ivy Lord was eleven years old when, with her family, she heard the declaration of war on the radio. She lived in Dagenham at the time. Many people went out into the street, most appearing dazed. People must have realized that war was possible, or even probable, but that announcement made it a reality. With her family Ivy went into the back garden where her father was still digging the foundations for the Anderson shelter. It certainly was not ready for use at that time. Then the siren sounded, but the majority of people stayed outside, still not quite believing what was happening. Fortunately the All Clear sounded before too long. It had been a false alarm, but nevertheless terrifying. The previous day there had been an interesting display of cakes in the nearby bakery. One woman was heard to say, 'I'll get those tomorrow.' Unfortunately the next day they all disappeared from the window, not to be seen again as long as the war lasted.

Pamela Harper, née Staples, lived in Brentwood and also remembers the memorable day of the war announcement. The family gathered around the radio and she recalls, as a nine-year-old, a feeling of excitement. Her parents remained very quiet. People did not talk about their fears in front of children in those days.

GOVERNMENT EVACUATION SCHEME

The Government have ordered evacuation of school children.

If your children are registered for evacuation send them to their assembly point at once.

If your children are not registered and you wish them to be evacuated, the teachers or the school keeper will help you.

If you do not wish your children to be evacuated you must not send them to school until further notice.

Posters notifying the arrival of parties in the country will be displayed at the schools at which the children assembled for evacuation.

An evacuation notice.

Pamela Harper in 2016. (F.J. Clamp)

Twins Ena and Una Felton also lived in Brentwood. They were five when the war started and remember carrying their gas masks in small cardboard boxes to St Thomas's School in Coptfold Road. They also each had a flat tin containing two biscuits and a rubber. The latter was to be popped into the mouth during a bad air raid to be bitten on in case of a bomb dropping nearby. The idea was that it would stop them from biting their tongues in shock. At school there were coal fires in the classrooms and occasionally, as a special treat, potatoes could be taken to school and placed underneath the fire where they baked and could be eaten later in the day.

Preparations for evacuation had already been made by the government and almost at once many Dagenham schools closed, with children and teachers leaving for places that were thought to be safer. However, Ivy's mother refused to let her go. She said, 'If we go we go together.' With her school closed and her friends away, the eleven-year-old later described this as the loneliest time of her life. A number of places of entertainment closed too, leaving the children remaining behind with little to occupy their time. Yet, as the 'Phoney War' continued without the expected invasion and relentless bombing that had been foretold, children began to return. By Christmas many were once more at home. Some mothers tried to organize lessons in their houses, but this was far from satisfactory. Slowly schools reopened, although a number of teachers were, by this time, involved in the forces or other war work.

Some, especially from London, had been sent away almost immediately. A number arrived in Essex and the Felton family had a boy from the city billeted with them. Apparently he had an enormous appetite and the twins insisted that he ate them out of 'house and home'. This must have been difficult at a time when food shortages were already being felt. At this time Brentwood County High School for Girls started to play its part in the war plans. It became a receiving centre for evacuees who arrived by train and were then billeted in houses around the town. The declaration of war had come towards the end of the summer holidays and an order was given that no school could re-open until adequate shelters for the pupils were provided. This resulted in workmen arriving to dig trenches to act as shelters but the staff were also called into service in a very different capacity. Every window had to be covered with 1½in strips of brown sticky tape in a criss-cross pattern. This was to avoid anyone being injured if the glass was shattered by a bomb blast.

The building also became a new school for children over eleven years of age from London. Three schools were sent to Brentwood; West Ham High School, West Ham Secondary School and Leytonstone County High School. The girls were billeted locally. Fortunately the nearby Ursuline Convent School stepped in and quickly took responsibility for West Ham High School. It was arranged that Brentwood girls should attend school on Monday, Wednesday and Friday and the other schools on Tuesday, Thursday and Saturday. This was far from being an ideal situation, but it worked. A major problem was the fact that a school built to house 450 girls suddenly acquired double that number. As the 'Phoney War' dragged on, many of the West Ham and Leytonstone pupils began to drift back home, although their own school buildings remained closed until well after Christmas. However, life at Brentwood County High School could return to some sort of normality.

In the north-east of the county Clacton, which had been developing as a popular seaside town between the wars, now found the holiday trade diminishing at an alarming rate. Instead the town received evacuees, many children from London. Some complained about the cleanliness of the children, especially as a number had nit-infested hair. The situation did not last for long. Being sent to the seaside must have been a dream come true for many of those children, but it was soon realized that east-coast towns were extremely vulnerable. The evacuees were sent elsewhere, to areas considered to be safer, as were many of the local children.

Pamela Harper recalls the arrival of evacuees almost as soon as war was declared. She had been out for the day with her family and as they arrived home they found a group of people at the end of their road looking for a billet for a mother who was carrying a baby. They agreed to take them in, but there was a problem. They had nothing with them to use for the baby. Fortunately Pamela had a doll's pram which proved to be just the right size for the baby, although sleeping arrangements were a problem. The house had three bedrooms but to reach the third bedroom it was necessary to pass through the second one. Luckily, during the war, people managed to find solutions to all sorts of problems and the family coped.

An armoured vehicle on Rainham Marshes. (With thanks to The Ford Motor Company)

Things might have looked brighter for the agricultural community, but not for seaside towns. As we have seen those that had flourished during the inter-war years now faced problems. Once the air-raids started fewer people wanted to travel, especially to the east coast. It was too close to Europe for comfort. Southend-on-Sea also found the holiday trade declining and later many of the hotels were requisitioned for naval personnel. Similarly Harwich faced new problems. During the years of the Depression there had been a population shift towards nearby Dovercourt. As the war started many empty houses were turned into billets as servicemen were sent to the town.

On 9 September 1939 Southend Pier was closed to the public. It was taken over by the Royal Navy and was re-named HMS *Leigh*. The seafront was also re-named and became HMS *Westcliff*. During the war the pier, although vulnerable to attack, was left complete as it was used as a mustering point for convoys. In all 3,367 convoys involving 84,297 ships departed from Southend-on-Sea. The pier also served as the Naval Control Base for the Thames Estuary. Throughout the war many of the large houses and hotels above the cliffs were taken over by the Royal Navy.

Harwich is linked to one of the first casualties of the war, HMS *Gypsy*, a 'G' class destroyer that had been launched in 1936. Before the war the ship had been part of the Mediterranean Fleet. Then, with the start of hostilities she was transferred to escort duties in British waters. On 21 November 1939 HMS *Gypsy* rescued three German airman from outside Harwich harbour. She returned to hand them over to the military and then again set off to sea. That was when disaster struck. She set off a magnetic mine just outside the harbour. It was reported that the ensuing explosion shook the whole town. As the explosion happened close to shore it was possible to rescue 115 crew members, but thirty died, including the captain. Had the plane from which the three German airmen came been responsible for laying the mine? There were rumours, but no one knew for certain.

The government expected an immediate mass air attack, and hospitals were prepared and mortuaries issued with cardboard coffins ready for the thousands of expected fatalities. Fortunately they were unnecessary. Instead endless new regulations were introduced. Everyone was expected to carry a luggage label showing their name and address. Identity cards were promised shortly. Recalling the problems caused by unshielded lights during the previous war, shops, homes and public buildings were expected to observe a blackout at night. Vehicles were made to drive with dimmed headlights. However, road deaths were reported to have doubled, so the restrictions had to be eased to an extent. Headlamps had to be covered with cardboard with just 2in holes left for light to show. Blackout curtaining quickly disappeared from shops and householders were advised to paint the edges of windows black so no chink of light could be seen outside. Soon wardens patrolled, looking out for any signs of stray light and those found guilty of not observing the blackout could be heavily fined. Many churches, with their large windows, had to abandon evening services or move them to the afternoon. Not so St Mary's, Prittlewell. The vicar organized the making of enormous blinds of shiny black material. It was the job of the church wardens to hoist them up before a service and to make sure that every window was safely covered. Later the blinds were lowered, rolled up and left on the pews ready for the next service. A zigzag screen protected the porch to ensure that no light escaped.

St Mary's Church, Prittlewell. (F.J. Clamp)

Selo was a major employer in Brentwood. This photographic company was perhaps better known for Ilford Films. Ilford was the town chosen by the company in 1879, in an effort to find a dust-free environment for the production of photographic plates and later film. However, by 1899 conditions had changed and the town was no longer dust-free. Instead land was bought in Brentwood in 1901 and here the company flourished. The factory was requisitioned for use as a store in the Great War. Once the factory was returned to private ownership in 1921 the company started producing films of high quality including rolls, colour, cine and X-ray film. When war came once more in 1939 Selo began producing film suitable for aerial reconnaissance, an invaluable contribution to the war effort.

By early September Winston Churchill was once again appointed First Lord of the Admiralty and he became a member of the War Cabinet. Anthony Eden was also recalled to the government to be Secretary of State for Dominion Affairs. Much to the delight of the

British Australia, New Zealand and Canada loyally declared war on Germany.

Although the expected air offensive had not happened, by early October 250,000 more conscripts were called up. Later in the month newspaper readers were horrified to learn that as many as 800 men were believed to have died when the battleship HMS *Royal Oak* was sunk by a German submarine in her home base of Scapa Flow. Also, on the same day, the first enemy planes reached Britain. This happened on the Firth of Forth when the naval base at Rosyth was attacked. U-boats were also attacking more British shipping, but it was claimed that approximately thirty of the enemy craft had been shot down.

In late October Germany proposed that all Jews should be made to wear a yellow Star of David. By the end of the month the British public learned of the imprisonment of Jews in concentration camps, a horror that was to continue throughout the war.

With the official declaration of war Essex airfields prepared themselves for the expected air attacks. Blenheims of the Auxiliary Air

HSL 102, used by the RAF to rescue airmen from the sea. (F.J. Clamp)

Force 600 (City of London) Squadron arrived at RAF Hornchurch just hours before the start of the war. They were intended for night flying and often changed their base between Hornchurch, Southend, Manston and Northolt. Much of their work involved flying over the Thames Estuary, especially as Heinkel He 115 floatplanes were regularly dropping mines there. Supermarine Spitfires had moved to Hornchurch in 1938 and they were flown with great enthusiasm by their pilots.

There were some nuisance raids, but not the mass attacks that had been expected. To stay prepared and ready there was regular formation practice. This 'Phoney War' was a time of anti-climax lasting from September 1939 until May of the following year. Although Britain did not see a great deal of action at first, the German army continued to make considerable advances on the Continent.

Sadly, in this time of heightened tension, there were some disasters. One of these happened on the third day of the war. 74 Squadron was scrambled from Hornchurch with orders to intercept enemy raiders who had apparently reached Essex. Communications in those early days of war were still rather primitive. The raiders were actually Hurricanes from 56 Squadron flying from North Weald. Later this became known as 'The Battle of Barking Creek'. Two Hurricanes were shot down, one pilot being killed and the other injured. A court martial followed but the two pilots involved were later acquitted. What was later described as 'friendly fire' often had disastrous results.

74 Squadron was frequently dispatched from Hornchurch to RAF Rochford. While it was still at Hornchurch Flying Officer W.E. Measures destroyed one of the first German planes to reach the English mainland. This happened on 20 November 1939 when it was shot down over the sea 15 miles off Southend. As one of the nearest airfields to Europe Hornchurch was later to play a vital part in the Battle of Britain.

In mid-November the price of petrol was increased by one and a half pence per gallon. In future it would cost one shilling and nine pence halfpenny. The 'Phoney War' dragged on, but a new menace was threatening shipping. Magnetic mines could be laid by craft like the small, fast E-Boats or dropped by parachute. The Thames Estuary was an area often targeted. This brought the menace of war ever closer to the Essex coast. On 18 November the Dutch liner *Simon Bolivar*, en route from Holland to the West Indies, set off a magnetic mine just 12 miles from Walton-on-the-Naze. There were many casualties as the

War graves at St Andrew's Church, Hornchurch. (F.J. Clamp)

ship sank quickly. Vessels were dispatched to pick up survivors and 300 of the 400 passengers and crew were saved. They were taken to Harwich and then sent to local hospitals and to those in the surrounding towns. Later in the month the Japanese steamer *Terukuni Maru* was also sunk as a result of enemy action. She had been on her way to London. The Walton lifeboat was launched but the passengers and crew had already been rescued by the Trinity House vessel *Alert*. The war was getting ever closer. One fortunate result came following the dropping of a German parachute mine close to Shoeburyness. It was recovered at low tide and deactivated. The Royal Navy's Mine Warfare Section then had an opportunity to examine the mine and discover its secrets. As a result it was possible to alter the magnetic signature of all vessels, making it safer to travel by sea. In December 1939 rationing was introduced for both bacon and butter and shortly after Christmas this was extended to include sugar and meat. Every family in the country would begin to feel the true hardships of war.

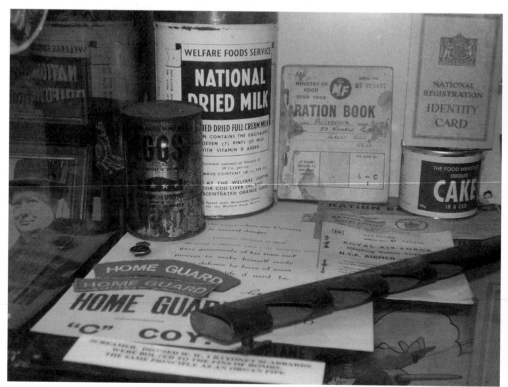

Ration book and tinned food. (With thanks to Canvey Bay Museum)

In Great Britain it might have been known as the 'Phoney War', but this was not the case in mainland Europe. The 158,000-strong BEF landed in France with 25,000 vehicles to bolster the French defences. Their movements in Britain had been carefully controlled with small units travelling only at night. This was to avoid air attacks. For some weeks in advance of this movement RAF planes had been making reconnaissance flights over Europe. Troops also left for the Middle East. In Prague nine Czech students were executed by the Nazis for involvement in anti-German demonstrations.

December 1939 saw increasing food shortages, but the fear of mass air attacks faded. In London art treasures had been removed from the National Gallery to be stored somewhere in Wales. Their exact destination was not disclosed. Myra Hess drew large audiences to her lunchtime concerts and in the West End some of the theatres that had closed on the declaration of war now reopened. As the old year faded there was hope that the coming one would see an improvement in life generally and a belief that perhaps peace might soon return.

CHAPTER TWO

1940

Britain at Bay

By 1940 two million nineteen to twenty-seven-year-olds had been called up for military service, mainland Europe saw an increase in enemy aggression and the weather deteriorated throughout the first month. On 17 January the River Thames froze, the first time since 1888. Rationing now became a serious problem for all. Butter, sugar, bacon and ham could only be bought with the use of ration books. Four ounces of butter and twelve ounces of sugar were allowed per week. Uncooked bacon or ham were both restricted to four ounces per week. If the bacon or ham had been cooked the allowance was reduced to three and a half ounces per week. At this stage coupons were not needed for food purchased in restaurants or canteens, as long as the meal was consumed on the premises. However, those staying in hotels or guest houses needed to hand over their ration books to the proprietor for the duration of their stay. Any euphoria felt at the end of the previous year quickly faded as the reality of the harsh winter took hold.

Alma Baker, née Sproggs, was an eleven-year-old living in Dagenham when the war broke out. She had just passed the Scholarship and had a place at the new technical college where she studied Commerce and learnt shorthand and typing. Many children from the area were to be evacuated as the fear of invasion grew. The students were told to report to school each day with a small bag of clothes, some food and money. Then, one Wednesday, a message appeared on the school notice board announcing that the evacuation day was to be on Friday. On Thursday Alma did not take her emergency supplies to school, but suddenly orders came through that they were to leave on that day. Her mother was shopping near the school when the butcher

A reconstructed Second World War shop. (With thanks to The Royal Gunpowder Mills)

told her that the children were about to leave, instead of on Friday. He had heard that they were all lined up and ready to go to the station. The butcher lent her some money and she raced away to buy essentials for her daughter. Alma was in a long line when her mother arrived and shared out the food she had bought between her daughter and her friends. There was also a little money for each of them. Alma recalls being mortified when her mother kissed her goodbye in front of the line of children!

The group walked to Upney station and after a long journey by steam train they finally arrived in Weston-super-Mare. Her life as an evacuee was interesting. With a friend Alma first went to an elderly couple, but the wife was never seen as she was apparently delicate and spent all her time in her sitting room. There were no places left in the schools in Weston and they were soon transferred to Street where their

A child's gas mask (centre). (With thanks to Canvey Bay Museum)

own teachers taught them for half of each day and the other half was spent on non-academic subjects. Later they moved to the home of the grandmother of the Clarks' shoe family, which was quite a culture shock for two girls from Dagenham. The house was large, and there were prayers in the library each morning as the family were Quakers, with the staff attending too. There was no air-raid shelter so they all crouched under the library table during raids. After two more moves they finally returned to Dagenham in 1942.

Early in January Australia pledged aircraft and 3,000 airmen to aid the Allies and in February the first squadron arrived in Britain from the Royal Canadian Air Force. In France the Germans gained ground to the north of Paris. At sea the number of casualties grew as mines took their toll and attacks were also made from the air. When a Union Castle liner hit a mine off the south-east coast, 152 people were feared dead. In late February it was reported that German U-Boat commanders had been ordered to attack all neutral ships as well as those of the Allies. This resulted in fewer ships calling at British ports. Food supplies from overseas therefore became even more limited

In March general meat rationing was also introduced, although offal, rabbit, poultry, game, fish, brawn, sausages and pies were not rationed at that stage. Ivy Lord from Dagenham recalled that her family and most of her neighbours kept chickens. As eggs became scarce those who kept chickens were not able to buy them. Instead they were issued with an allowance of chicken feed.

Alan Parrish, his mother and sister were evacuated to Clevedon early in the war. Their hosts were unwelcoming and after only a few weeks the family returned home to Essex. However, by July 1940 the Luftwaffe started intensive bombing of the south of England. Alan was again evacuated, this time to Dunmow. He stayed in a farmhouse in an idyllic country setting. He finally returned home at the end of the London Blitz.

The first British civilian died in an air raid in March, which must have increased the fear that similar attacks would happen throughout the country. The 'Phoney War' made many feel that they were safe from attack, but such reports brought the true reality of war ever closer. There was constant activity at the Essex airfields. Sixty Spitfires were based at Hornchurch. Sadly twenty-two of them did not survive the war.

By May 1940 everything changed. The 'Phoney War' ended and the full reality of the conflict with Germany hit everyone in Britain. The same month there was deep shock in Clacton when a Heinkel bomber crashed on a house in Victoria Road. The plane had apparently become lost in fog off the east coast. It carried two mines, intended for the shipping lanes. It had been hit earlier, but not destroyed, by anti-aircraft guns positioned near Harwich. It then flew over Clacton, and circled for half an hour, hoping to find a landing place. Instead it crashed on the home of Frederick and Dorothy Gill, both of whom died. There was a huge explosion. Over 160 people were injured in the blast and thirty-four of those were registered as serious. Sixty-seven houses were damaged, although a nearby air-raid shelter remained intact.

As the site was examined rescuers found what they believed was a hot-water tank. Later it was noticed that the 'tank' had German writing on the side. This was identified as an unexploded parachute mine and

Nurses at the Southend-on-Sea ARP centre. (With thanks to Brenda Sowerby)

was defused by Royal Naval mine-disposal officers. A second one had exploded at the crash site. These early-war fatalities were caused not by intentional bombing of civilians, but by a very unfortunate accident.

Another evacuee from Dagenham was Ada Lapaer, née Lucas. With her mother and four siblings she, like Alma Sproggs, was sent to Weston-super-Mare. The children's father was serving in the Royal Navy. The family was sent to a hotel where the basement was for their everyday use, but their sole bedroom was in the attic on the eleventh floor. There were no lifts and her two-month-old sister slept in her pram. This had to be manhandled up and down the stairs each day. It was not a happy experience and before long they returned home. Later Ada, with her eight-year-old brother, was sent to Devon. Just two weeks after they once more returned home, the house in which they had lived during their evacuation was completely destroyed in a bombing raid. A little later in the war Ada's family were living in Ilchester Road, Dagenham. She vividly recalls a plane flying straight along the road dropping incendiary bombs. A sheet of flame could be seen in the middle of the road and some of the houses were damaged.

On 10 May Chamberlain resigned as Prime Minister and his place was taken by Winston Churchill, who immediately started establishing a coalition government. Germany had invaded Holland and, although the French and her allies reacted, they were too late. The German army had already crossed most of Holland. Various unsuccessful counter-attacks followed. On 20 May the German army reached the coast and the BEF was cut off from the armies of France and Belgium. The German generals believed that, if the Allies reached the coast, there would be no escape and they would be at the mercy of the Luftwaffe's bombs. At this point the enemy decided to halt their advance towards Dunkirk for three days to consolidate their forces. But for this decision the outcome would almost certainly have been very different. In fact it gave the Allies time to organize the evacuation from Dunkirk. Drastic action was needed.

John Garrod in naval uniform. (With thanks to Joan Green)

It was on 27 May that many of those involved with small boats around the country received telephone messages from the small craft section of the British Ministry of Shipping. It was known that only boats with a shallow draft would be capable of reaching the beaches of Dunkirk and these were the ones needed by the Ministry. They would be able to navigate in the shallow waters. Along the Thames yachts, pleasure boats and launches were moored. Similar craft were to be found around the south and east coasts. Fishing boats were also ideal. Many of the boats were taken with permission from the owners, but others were requisitioned if owners could not be contacted, because time was short. After checks to ensure that the boats were seaworthy they were taken to Ramsgate ready for the crossing to Dunkirk. Most of the owners did not man their own boats. This task was performed by naval officers, ratings and experienced volunteers. Fishermen and other professional sailors were able to take their own craft across the Channel.

It is impossible to follow the stories of all the small Essex and Thames boats that undertook the journey to France. Instead we will look at three. *Endeavour* was one of the Leigh-on-Sea Cockle Bawley boats that set out at 0030 hours on 31 May for Southend-on-Sea. From there they crossed the Channel. *Endeavour*'s captain was F. Hall and she joined a convoy of small ships commanded by a Royal Navy lieutenant. Close to the French coast they were spotted by the Luftwaffe, but RAF planes gave protection and the *Endeavour* and the other cockle boats with her were able to continue with their mission. She picked up troops from the beach and later from the East Mole where others had gathered. These grateful soldiers were then transported to larger ships, ready for the journey back to England. She also rescued men from the inner harbour. Although her rudder was smashed at some point she returned to Ramsgate, being towed across the Channel by *Ben & Lucy*, a coaster. Later Admiral Sir Bertram Ramsey, commander of the Dunkirk operation, commented on the 'exemplary conduct of the crews of the cockle boats'. He pointed out that they were all volunteers who had never before been under fire and, apart from one of the crews, had not previously been further from home waters than Ramsgate. Sadly one of the Leigh fishing boats struck a mine and the crew of four perished. *Endeavour* is the only survivor of the Leigh-built fishing boats that took part in the Dunkirk evacuation. It is registered with the Association of Little Ships and is cared for by the *Endeavour* Trust of Leigh-on-Sea.

Another vessel involved in the Dunkirk rescue was *Crested Cock*. She was a steam tug and her master, Captain T. Hills, wrote an account of her exploits at that time. She left home at 5.15 pm on 29 May bound for Tilbury Dock Basin and towing three sailing barges. From there she sailed first to Southend-on-Sea and then to Ramsgate. Orders were then given to proceed to Dover. Finally, at 4 am on 30 May 1940 she left for Dunkirk towing a lighter loaded with fresh water, supplies and troops. Captain Hills anchored 60ft from the beach and the troops went ashore. *Crested Cock* was then dispatched to help a destroyer, HMS *Impulsive*, which needed urgent assistance. Troops were already on board, but a damaged propeller meant that she was unable to turn and take them to safety. *Crested Cock* managed to turn her around and the destroyer then proceeded on just one propeller. The steam tug escorted her to Dunkirk Pier. All this took place under continual shelling and

A school group at Leigh-on-Sea. The windows are protected with tape. (With thanks to Lois Holmes)

heavy bombing. *Crested Cock* then returned to Dover but on 1 June she went to aid another destroyer, HMS *Worcester*, which had been in a collision. Some of the troops on board were in the water so the steam tug helped with their rescue. Later she returned to Dunkirk to rescue anything and anyone needing rescuing. Finally the crew returned to Dover after an unforgettable few days.

Unfortunately misunderstandings sometimes occurred. Lifeboats were called into service and on 30 May the RNLI contacted eighteen of its stations in south-east England with instructions to send their lifeboats to Dover, fully loaded with fuel, a full crew and towing hawsers. The *E.M.E.D.*, a 'Watson' class lifeboat from Walton-on-the-Naze, was soon on its way. The crew members were expecting to sail with their craft but there had apparently been a misunderstanding. The first lifeboat men to arrive were informed that Royal Navy crews were assigned to take over their boats. Instead of leaving for France these experts at sea rescue from Walton, with others, were issued with travel warrants and told to return home. The *E.M.E.D.* left for France on 31 May under the command of Lieutenant R. Mead RNVR. Her exact movements at Dunkirk are not recorded but sadly Lieutenant Mead was killed during the operation.

Essex men and boats had played their part in the evacuation from Dunkirk. Many died in the horrific conditions of battle, but others bravely served under continual fire, bringing back the beleaguered troops from the beaches. Was it a victory or a defeat? The debate goes on, but Winston Churchill, with his amazing gift of oratory, persuaded the country of the former and all those involved had reason to feel immense pride in their achievements during those terrifying days. Certainly the army had retreated, but because of the bravery of those involved in the rescue they were able to regroup and fight again.

We sometimes forget the vital role played by the RAF during the Dunkirk evacuation. As Holland fell to the German onslaught British

A flying jacket. (With thanks to North Weald Airfield Museum)

planes gave support and many were lost. As France came under threat from the enemy advance the British government was put under pressure to send ever more replacements from Fighter Command. However, Air Chief Marshal Sir Hugh Dowding, head of Fighter Command, insisted that no Spitfire squadrons should be used in this way. He realized that if and when France fell, Britain would be next and every Spitfire would then be needed. This must have been an extremely frustrating time for the pilots based at Hornchurch with three squadrons of the iconic planes. Yet on 16 May they were called upon to fly to France as the BEF retreated. They harried the enemy planes at every opportunity, although those fighting on the ground did not always realize the sterling support that was being given. On 21 May 74 Squadron was involved in a dogfight over Dunkirk and six enemy planes were destroyed. Those returning to base in Hornchurch reported on the chaotic scenes below.

Every day from 21 May until 6 June Essex-based airmen were involved in flying to France to give all the support they could. At the close of 24 May Air Chief Marshal Dowding sent a signal to the four Hornchurch Spitfire Squadrons congratulating them on their work that day. Thirty-seven enemy aircraft had been shot down with small loses on the British side. Both men and planes were lost during those horrendous days, but those at Hornchurch remained positive. In all Fighter Command lost 229 aircraft and 128 pilots during Operation Dynamo, as the Dunkirk operation was known. A total of 2,739 sorties was flown during those momentous days. Twenty-three pilots from Hornchurch were lost. Time was needed to recover.

June 27th saw five Hornchurch pilots ready to receive recognition for their efforts. There was a ceremonial parade and it was known that someone special was to make the presentation to the five. Air Chief Marshal Dowding attended, along with Air Marshal Nichol and Air Marshal W.C. Fielden. The identity of the very special visitor was unknown until a large car arrived on the tarmac and King George VI stepped out. The five pilots were: Squadron Leader J.A. Leathart of 54 Squadron who received the Distinguished Service Order, Flight Lieutenant R.R.S. Tuck of 65 Squadron, Flight Lieutenant A.G. Malan of 74 Squadron, Flight Lieutenant A.C. Deere of 54 Squadron and Pilot Officer J.R. Allen. The latter four all received the Distinguished Flying Cross. This was a very proud moment in the life of this very active airfield.

A replica Hawker Hurricane Mk 1 to be seen near the main gates at North Weald Airfield. (F.J. Clamp)

The evacuation of Dunkirk might be over, but the trials of the French were not. By 14 June the Nazi swastika was flying from the Eiffel Tower and the Arc de Triomphe. On 22 June a French delegation went to the forest of Compiègne to sign an armistice agreement in the same railway carriage that was used in November 1918 for the surrender of the Germans. Britain was now fighting alone, but still supported by her Commonwealth allies. The summer of 1940 saw the start of the Battle of Britain. At first the Luftwaffe concentrated on attacking coastal shipping and convoys. This soon changed, with Hitler demanding that Fighter Command be eliminated before a full-scale invasion of Britain was launched. This would especially affect the Essex airfields. There were seven main sector stations covering the south-east of England: Hornchurch, Biggin Hill, Debden, Kenley, Northolt, North Weald and Tangmere. Of these Hornchurch was the only one to have three squadrons of Spitfires. The airfield had fifty of these aircraft.

Southend had first been used as a landing field for the Royal Flying Corps during the Great War and it played a very useful role at that time. Then, with the outbreak of the Second World War, it was requisitioned by the Air Ministry and became an important fighter station with Spitfires and Hurricanes. It had the disadvantage of being difficult to defend, the main fear being that enemy paratroopers might invade. The surrounding land was comparatively flat and therefore ideal for attack by parachutists. To counteract this problem a number of pillboxes were erected. These were of many shapes and sizes and between the runways retractable Picket-Hamilton pillboxes were put in place. It is believed as many as fifty pillboxes surrounded the airfield.

The whole area was well defended and ready to engage German bombers on their way to London. When they crossed the coast at

The church on Foulness Island. (F.J. Clamp)

Foulness they would encounter 3.7in guns at Fisherman's Head, Ridgemont Farm and New Burwood. Some shells could reach over 23,000ft. Next the bombers encountered more gunfire at Great Wakering and Sutton. There were also batteries at Hawkwell and Rayleigh. Despite these problems attacks continued and all the airfields had to be constantly on the alert.

Following the evacuation from Dunkirk Britain prepared itself for invasion. With its long coastline, comparatively flat terrain and easy access to both London and the Midlands it was realized that Essex was especially vulnerable to attack. Enemy tanks and armoured vehicles would be able to move swiftly inland. A solution was urgently required. 'Stop Lines' were suggested. There were to be lines of defence based on rivers, marshes or woodland, in fact anywhere that could slow an invasion until reinforcements arrived. At first temporary barriers were erected, but these were quickly replaced with more substantial defences to impede the progress of any invaders. Ditches could be dug to stop tanks and work started throughout the county on concrete pillboxes that would protect these trenches. Gun emplacements were also constructed, as well as rifle pits and anti-tank barriers. Narrow, shallow rivers might also be easy to cross by invading troops so many were widened and made deeper with bridges blocked or even mined. A number of trees were removed as they could give cover to invading forces.

What was known as the General Headquarters Line came into Essex from Cambridge. It then followed the River Chelmer before continuing around Chelmsford on its way to the River Thames. Essex saw many of these defensive structures being built, especially along the coast and rivers. At the time of writing six Second World War Heritage Trails have been set up across the county. Information boards explain the various remains that may be seen, many still in good condition, although others have long since disappeared. Now many are hidden by undergrowth and bushes. At Walton-on-the-Naze two have fallen onto the beach from the top of the cliffs as the area is subject to constant coastal erosion. They can still be seen, under water when the tide comes in, but close enough to the shore to be reached on foot when the water recedes. They each originally contained an anti-aircraft machine gun that was placed in a sunken well. The gunner would be hidden from view. It is believed that Lewis guns from the previous war had been brought out of storage for use at Walton.

A pillbox at Walton-on-the-Naze. (F.J. Clamp)

The method of construction of pillboxes is interesting. Inner and outer walls were usually constructed using wooden planking and leaving a gap between the two. Concrete was then poured in to fill the space. Once this was set the planking could be removed and re-used for the next pillbox. The pattern of the horizontal planks may still be seen on the outer walls of some of the pillboxes. Sometimes corrugated iron or patterned steel sheeting was used inside but it was unable to be removed when the concrete set and can still be seen on some internal walls. There were many different types of pillboxes but they generally fall into two types – infantry and artillery. One of the former that survives at Walton was designed to hold a squad of men with rifles and machine guns. Tett Turrets were rare and were designed to be used by a single man. The former RAF Hornchurch airfield still has surviving examples of these structures. When one of them was excavated for the BBC programme *Two Men in a Trench* the original crawl was unearthed and also a pair of Second World War goggles.

A former gun emplacement, once on the cliffs at Walton-on-the-Naze. (F.J. Clamp)

The Tett Turret at the former RAF Hornchurch airfield. (F.J. Clamp)

The number of Anderson shelters was increasing. Ena and Una Felton remember the first night spent in theirs in the back garden. It was cold and full of condensation and their mother decided that it would be better to stay in the house, rather than risk catching pneumonia in the shelter. The family had a large, sturdy oak dining table and it was under this that the family gathered during air raids and the children often slept. The Anderson shelter was used for storing apples and potatoes as the atmosphere would keep them cool. The girls went to St Thomas' School, Brentwood. In the playground there was an underground shelter with benches along the sides and duck boards to keep feet dry as the ground often became very damp. There were also brick-built shelters above ground, although what protection these would have given if there had been a direct hit is doubtful.

Una and Ena Felton in 2016. (F.J. Clamp)

One of their neighbours, Pamela Harper, née Staples, also remembers the Anderson shelter in the garden. On her first visit water collected on the floor and this affected her younger brother's asthma. As a result the shelter was only used once more during the hostilities.

Instead they slept under the dining-room table. This was pushed up against the piano to give extra room for their feet.

In the past Britain had prided itself on its navy, convinced that any sea attacks could be repelled. Yet by 1940 it was realized that the worst attacks were likely to come from the air. The first bomb to fall in Brentwood was dropped in July 1940. This hit The Goldings in Great Warley, previously the home of Evelyn Heseltine and his family. It has since been extended and has become the De Rougemont Manor Hotel. Other Essex towns were also being bombed and once again thoughts turned to the evacuation of children. In the summer of 1940 it was decided to evacuate a number of schools from areas believed to be vulnerable to attack. St Mary's Church of England Primary School in Prittlewell, near Southend-on-Sea, was one of those affected. Southend was seen as a likely target. Shoeburyness Barracks were to be found to the east, Rochford Aerodrome to the north, the longest pleasure pier in the world to the south and London to the west. Bombers going to the city would often pass over Southend and any bombs left after a raid were likely to be dropped on the town.

Pamela Winn was a six-year-old pupil at St Mary's School and her parents decided that she should join the evacuees, and take her three-year-old sister Frances with her. Carrying their gas masks in their small brown cardboard boxes over one shoulder and a small case or haversack containing a minimum of essential clothes and food for their journey, a long crocodile set off for Prittlewell Railway Station. The children were packed into a train and their mothers watched from the platform. We often hear of parents who refused to let their children go, but it took a different type of courage to see your small offspring set off on a journey into the unknown, not knowing whether you would ever be reunited.

The school went to Huthwaite, a mining village on the Derbyshire-Nottinghamshire border. Foster parents assembled ready to select the children they wanted to join them. The sisters were fortunate to be kept together, as many siblings were sent to separate families. Some of the teachers had travelled with the children so lessons were able to continue in a local school. Like many others Pamela did not enjoy the experience, although Frances did, possibly because she admits she was thoroughly spoilt by the mining family they joined.

The Battle of Britain officially started on 10 July 1940. At first the

Reg Winn. (F.J. Clamp)

97, best Road
westcliff on Sea
Jan 29° 41

Dear Frances Joyce,

This is my first letter to my big girl who is now 4 yrs old. I wish that I could be with you on your birthday, but I will be thinking of you all the time, and hope that you have a lovely day. Plenty of presents, lots of nice games. Will you ask mummy to write and tell me all that you did. I expect that you will have on your party frock, and also Pam. Dont forget to let big boy Clive John join in with some of the smaller games, such as ring-a ring-a- roses. He likes that. Will you also ask Pam to write me another one of her nice letters. I should like that too. Once again a happy birthday, and ask Pam to give you four big kisses from daddy. Lots of Love.
                                    Daddy.

A letter from Reg Winn sent to his daughter during her evacuation. (F.J. Clamp)

Luftwaffe targeted coastal towns, of which the county had many. Shipping was also attacked. Next they moved on to attack airfields, the aim being to wipe out as many aircraft as possible. The Hurricane squadrons of North Weald quickly became involved, but the first raid on their home base took place on 24 August. It was reported that over 200 bombs fell on the airfield and also on the nearby village. A number of buildings were destroyed on the airfield and nine members of the Essex Regiment, attached to the airfield for ground defence, were among those killed. The village suffered badly. The old post office and the King's Head and the Woolpack, two pubs often frequented by airman, were badly damaged as were nearby houses. Water mains were hit and Miss Metcalf of Ongar Park Hall Farm was killed.

These attacks on airfields in south-east England continued into September with many aerial battles taking place over Essex. Both planes and pilots were lost. On 3 September the Luftwaffe again attacked North Weald. This happened as planes were taking off. Once more the damage was considerable. Five people were killed and thirty-nine injured, but the airmen continued to attack the enemy aircraft, especially as they moved towards London. Officially the Battle of Britain ended in mid-September but on 29 October North Weald airfield was again attacked with six dead and forty-two wounded. In all forty-one of the aircrew from North Weald and Stapleford died during those horrifying weeks and seventeen were killed on the ground. The heroism of those at the airfield has now become a legend in the story of the Battle of Britain.

The Blitz on Britain started on 7 September 1940. This was the time of sustained bombing of the United Kingdom by Germany and lasted for a period of 267 days. London was attacked on seventy-one separate occasions, but other cities suffered too. Birmingham, Liverpool and Plymouth were each attacked eight times and other cities were also targeted, including a devastating attack on Coventry. Although there was some daylight bombing later in October the majority of raids were made at night. In Essex it became usual to hear the drone of bombers flying towards the capital. Searchlights lit up the sky as attempts were made to pick out the attackers and during raids there was the constant sound of gunfire. After the attacks remaining bombs were dropped on the county as the enemy planes lightened their loads before once more crossing over the Channel. Many people at that time ignored the damp

'The Haven', a preserved Plotland cottage at Laindon. (F.J. Clamp)

they had previously experienced and moved back into their Anderson shelters.

To see how the London Blitz affected one area of Essex we need to go back to the late nineteenth century. Two major events happened at that time. In 1882 an Act of Parliament permitted the London, Tilbury and Southend Railway Company to construct a direct line from London to Southend. The line was completed in 1889 and included stations at Laindon and Pitsea. The second momentous event was largely caused by the weather. For some years agricultural land in south-east Essex had been falling into disuse. Then in the late 1870s and early 1880s hot weather meant the heavy clay soil cracked and became rock hard, making agriculture almost impossible. Also at this time cheap wheat from America began flooding the British market. More Essex land went out of production and farms were sold cheaply to anyone willing to buy. The villages of Basildon, Pitsea, Laindon and Vange were all affected by these problems. It was only after the war that Basildon developed as a New Town.

Land agents saw their chance and eagerly bought up the land. They then decided to divide up the former fields into narrow strips, some only 18ft wide, but the length varied according to position. With advertisements placed in newspapers and at railway stations they were then offered for sale. The land agents got together with the railway companies and cheap fares were offered to prospective purchasers. Auctions were held, usually between April and October when the countryside looked at its best. Free lunches and even champagne helped to entice buyers, often from London's East End. The plots furthest from the station were the cheapest as there were no made-up roads or services. However, many sites were snapped up, some to be forgotten, but others were at first used for Sunday camping. Later small shacks and bungalows sprang up.

With the coming of the war travel became more difficult and many of the dwellings were left uninhabited. Then came the Blitz. Houses were vulnerable in London's East End and, with their properties facing the possibility of overnight destruction, some of the owners of the plots

The original Anderson shelter in the garden of 'The Haven'. (F.J. Clamp)

decided that it would be safer to move into the comparative safety of what, by this time, was known as The Plotlands. Most homes lacked gas, electricity, mains water and sewage, but the owners felt that such hardships were better than facing the constant nightly prospect of bombing in the city. Unfortunately for some the dream of a safe haven was short-lived. Many of the German bombers returning to their bases followed a route between the River Thames and the Southend Arterial Road (A127). To lighten their loads any left-over bombs were dropped on buildings en route. By the end of the war twenty-four people in the area had been killed and ninety-two seriously injured. There were many more minor injuries and damaged properties.

The airfields of Essex rose to the challenge of the Blitz. At first the Luftwaffe had attempted to wipe out Fighter Command sector stations. Many Essex airfields faced the full fury of the enemy bombers, but then their tactics changed. Attention was turned to London with the horrendous nightly attacks on the city. Planes from the airfields around the county fought back and attempted to destroy the incoming aircraft. On 15 September it was claimed that 185 enemy aircraft were destroyed, but post-war research lowered this number to fifty-six, with the RAF losing twenty-six. Because of the large number of planes lost, collections were made to buy new ones. Brentwood has always been an excellent town for fundraising and within four weeks residents raised £6,100 (£5,500 was needed to buy a Spitfire). Appropriately it was named *Brentwood* and entered service on 7 December 1940. It flew with various squadrons throughout 1941, but crashed at Llandevenny Airfield in Wales. Although the pilot was unhurt the plane was damaged beyond repair.

By 1941, although bombing continued, many of the children once again returned home as the immediate threat of invasion diminished. Lessons resumed in their own schools, with some disruption when the siren sounded. Then everyone had to walk, not run, in a silent, orderly manner to the air-raid shelters in the playground.

Evacuation stories could be told around the whole of Essex. Many concerned children sent away from the county, although others came in. They were frequently sent to rural areas and they often came from London. Many had never before seen cows or sheep and they found the wide-open country spaces terrifying, much preferring the narrow urban streets where they were born.

A bunk bed inside 'The Haven' Anderson shelter. (F.J. Clamp)

In the final three months of 1940 life across Europe became ever more difficult. In Britain too there was the constant fear of attack, an increasing number of streets had gaps where houses and shops had been destroyed and, as Germany tightened its grip on Atlantic shipping, food shortages became ever more acute.

On 3 October Neville Chamberlain resigned from the government because of ill health. His retirement was brief as his death from cancer was announced in early November. He was seventy-one. He will always be remembered for the ill-fated Munich agreement with Hitler but his patriotism cannot be denied as he struggled to maintain peace.

In November the Blitz was felt by a number of Midland towns, the industrial heartland of the country. The beautiful mediaeval city of Coventry was devastated by a horrendous air attack. Later in the month Birmingham and other towns also felt the full impact of German bombing and at the end of the month both Liverpool and Southampton faced intensive attacks by the Luftwaffe. December saw no improvement in living conditions. With Christmas approaching it was suggested that carrots should be used as a substitute for imported dried fruit in the traditional puddings. Bananas, oranges and lemons had also disappeared from the shelves.

As 1940 drew to a close there was no respite from the continuous bombing. On the night of 29 December an intensive raid on London took place. Water mains were severed and at least 10,000 incendiary bombs fell. It was low tide on the Thames, so firemen were unable to get water from the river and the mains supply was unavailable. Later water was pumped in from more distant mains. Sadly a number of deaths were caused by the collapse of burning buildings. Firemen fought on bravely, surely doing one of the most dangerous jobs of the war. During the dying days of 1940 the 'Phoney War' was almost forgotten. Essex airfields faced numerous attacks and nightly bombing. There was the constant fear that the next bomb dropped might fall on you. Life for everyone had now changed for ever.

Bomb damage at the Fords' Dagenham plant. (With thanks to The Ford Motor Company)

CHAPTER THREE

1941

Defeats and Setbacks

By the start of 1941 any hope that the war would soon be over had disappeared. The full impact of the Blitz had been felt and London was still reeling from the impact of nightly bombing. After the disastrous air raid of 29 December 1940 the regulations concerning fire-watching were tightened. Firms failing to provide adequate cover could face a £100 fine.

There was continuous support from the Commonwealth countries. In January the Australians and British had a notable victory at Tobruk in North Africa. News of any victory was well received back at home, but the people of Essex still lived daily with the thought that there might be a full-scale invasion at any time. More pillboxes, trenches and gun emplacements appeared along the General Headquarters Line, ready to defend the country whenever necessary. The majority of these defences were manned by members of the Home Guard.

After the outbreak of war, many who were unable to fight for various reasons still wanted to be actively involved. There were those who had been in the Great War but were now too old to enlist, while others were in reserved occupations. These included teachers, doctors and others who were considered essential for the smooth running of life on the Home Front. Essex citizens were keen to take part in any way they could. Romford and Hornchurch had a Troop of the Legion of Frontiersmen. In March 1940 the *Daily Mirror* published a report on The County of Essex Volunteer Corps, describing it as 'this vanguard of Britain's part-time army'. The Lord Bishop of Chelmsford expressed a desire to see a town-guard of men aged forty to sixty. Finally on 14 May 1940 Anthony Eden, now Secretary of State for War,

A pillbox at Walton-on-the-Naze. (F.J. Clamp)

announced on radio the formation of the Local Defence Volunteers. He asked for British volunteers aged between seventeen and sixty-five to come forward. The response exceeded all expectations. In the first seven days 250,000 tried to sign up. By July the total had reached 1.5 million. At the end of July 1940 the volunteer groups became known as the Home Guard.

This massive response led to problems. Training and arming the new recruits was essential. Quickly Area, Zone and Group organizers were appointed. As uniforms were unavailable in those early days temporary armbands were supplied bearing the letters 'LDV'. Weapons were even more difficult to obtain. There were only 70,000 rifles in the entire country. A general appeal was made and 20,000 extra guns, rifles and revolvers were obtained, but the number fell far short of those needed. Improvisation was essential. Some of the weapons available were unusual to say the least. HMS *Victory* supplied pikes dating back to the Battle of Trafalgar. Blunderbusses, elephant guns and rifles from the Crimean War also came back into use. One Essex group became known as 'The Cutlass Platoon' as twenty-four of these weapons were brought into use. Chelmsford received a Hotchkiss gun still in parts. Unfortunately no instructions for assembly were included. These early problems remind us of the *Dad's Army* programmes, but slowly matters

An air-raid warden's helmet. (With thanks to Canvey Bay Museum)

improved. Some Essex farmers made sure their own 12-bore shotguns were in first-rate condition, but by the autumn half a million weapons arrived from Canada and the United States of America. These included Ross, Springfield and Remington rifles and Thompson sub-machine guns. Improvisation was no longer necessary.

Early on the volunteers' main duties were preparing for the arrival of enemy paratroopers and constructing and manning roadblocks. Before more pillboxes were ready further improvisation was needed. Farm equipment, old vehicles and barbed wire, all were used to deter any would-be invaders. Apparently redundant piles from Clacton pier were even used as part of the defences. Once new pillboxes and gun emplacements were built, the old barriers could be removed. Many of these new structures were close to the coast, rivers, railways, major roads and airfields. The Home Guard were ready for invasion, but it did not come. They did manage to capture some enemy airmen who bailed out over British soil and survivors who escaped from crashed planes. Once these men had been detained the Home Guard would wait until they could hand them over to professional soldiers. They also defended key targets like factories, ammunition stores and beaches.

Brenda Sowerby's father, George Dando, was in charge of the Air Raid Precautions (ARP) Rescue Party at the Bournemouth Park Road Headquarters in Southend. This was centred on the school, which still stands. He had earlier qualified as a pit manager but during the war was working in the offices of the Gas Light and Coke Company based

Molly and George Dando in front of a wartime ambulance. (With thanks to Brenda Sowerby)

in York Road. The headquarters was also the centre for nurses and nursing auxiliaries. Ambulances were there, ready for sudden calls to emergencies. Molly McCardle was one of the nursing auxiliaries and it was here that she and George met. They married in June 1941 at St Mary's Church, Prittlewell. Prior to her marriage Molly had run a high-class milliners in St Helens Road Westcliff. During the war hats, like other clothes, were very basic so exclusive models were no longer needed.

The Bournemouth Park Unit went out to newly bombed houses. One of their jobs was to clear the properties of any possessions that might otherwise be stolen. These were then taken back to the ARP centre for later collection. Molly and George moved into a house in Wimborne Road. The previous owner had been a builder and they discovered a large air-raid shelter constructed under the lawn.

Bad weather caused considerable problems at airfields early in 1941. Snow was the major concern with a number of blizzards re-covering runways almost as soon as they were cleared. Flying became difficult or impossible under these conditions. At Hornchurch the role of the squadrons began to change from defence to attack. The aim was no longer just to defend the country, but to take the war to the enemy. This was good for the morale of all those involved. More land around the airfield was taken over and Sutton's Farm disappeared as new dispersal bays were built. One still survives and is used as a car park for the country park that now occupies part of the old site. By February the weather improved and more flights were possible. These came at a cost. Six pilots based at Hornchurch were lost during that month.

Food rationing caused concern throughout the country. Advice on how to adapt old recipes was given on the radio and books such as *A Kitchen Goes to War* were produced. There was concern felt about those selling on the black market who charged excessive prices for goods in short supply. Wholesalers and retailers were forbidden to sell certain items at higher prices than those charged the previous year. New price controls were introduced in an attempt to deal with this problem. Poultry, pickles, coffee, rice, cocoa, spaghetti, biscuits, custard and jelly all had their prices frozen. Prices mattered. Even a slight increase could badly affect the average working-class family with many living on an average weekly budget of less than £5 per week. Substitutes were often used. In Peggy Hutchinson's *Homemade Wine* book it was

The grave of Flight Sergeant N.R. Hollege, a twenty-two-year-old pilot at Hornchurch. (F.J. Clamp)

suggested that shredded wheat could be used as a substitute for wheat in recipes and Sarah Cutter of Prittlewell always mixed together the butter and margarine ration in a large bowl. In this way everyone in the family received some butter, which she firmly believed was healthier than margarine.

In the First World War the role of women had changed completely. They worked as nurses and nursing auxiliaries, delivered the post, cleaned trains, became bus conductors and worked in factories, including those dealing with highly dangerous explosives. However, once the war ended, many found that their new independence was removed and they returned to their old roles of housekeeping and cooking. Yet, as an ever-increasing number of men were again called

More bomb damage at Fords. (With thank to The Ford Motor Company)

up for military service, it became obvious that women were once more needed to fill the positions previously only held by men.

Some enlisted in the forces but in March 1941 the Minister of Labour, Ernest Bevin announced the first part of his plan to mobilize this untapped work force. Registration of twenty and twenty-one-year-old women would begin in April. The idea was that they would fill the vacancies left in industry and the auxiliary services. There was a particular need to have shell-filling factories working around the clock. Mr Bevin said, 'I cannot offer them a delightful life. I want them to come forward in the spirit that they are going to suffer some inconvenience but with a determination to help us through.' At that time married women with young children were exempt from this type of work, but if they could be employed locally there was to be an expansion of day and night nurseries and child-minding schemes. There was also a drive for men of forty-one and over to become trainees in factories. Unfortunately there was still a huge difference in pay for men and women. Male trainees received £3.0s 6d whilst their female colleagues received only £1.18s per week.

The Royal Gunpowder Mills at Waltham Abbey have been in existence since the 1850s. During the first two years of the Second World War the Mills were important for the production of cordite. They were also the sole producers of RDX, a component of Torpex, the explosive used in the famous 'Bouncing Bomb'. Many women worked on the production line. As a young unmarried woman Babs Haywood was sent to Leigh Bridge Industries on the Southend Arterial Road. This had become a barrage-balloon factory. The balloons were made in two parts and were later stitched together on machines. One of her jobs was to stick the two parts together before they were sewn. She had to sit on the floor, flatten the material and then put on glue to fix the pieces together. An opening was left so the balloon could be partly inflated. At that point someone went inside to test the seams. Babs recalled her journey home by bus. No one wanted to sit near those who had worked on the balloons because they still smelt strongly of glue. When the company finished making their quota of balloons they moved on to producing inflatable dinghies, but Babs was no longer required. Instead she moved on to train as a sheet metal worker, a job that would have been unheard-of for a woman before the war. Unfortunately she picked up an infection from the metal and was forced to leave, later joining the Women's Auxiliary Air Force as a wireless operator. When the war broke out Audrey Dudley had ambitions to join the Land Army. She was considered to be unsuitable as she was small and thought not to be robust enough for work on the land. Instead she joined the Ekco radio company in Southend. They were responsible for making the radios used in Lancaster bombers.

In 1939 60 per cent of the food consumed in Great Britain was imported from abroad. With knowledge gained from the previous conflict it was realized that ships carrying goods to this country would soon be blockaded or sunk. Homegrown food supplies had to be dramatically increased. In Essex there was a considerable amount of uncultivated land and farmers were encouraged to bring it into production as quickly as possible. There were monetary incentives and the threat of punishment for those who failed to comply. Problems

Babs Haywood working on a barrage balloon at Leigh-on-Sea. (F.J. Clamp)

arose once hostilities began when able-bodied young men were called up. This included many farm workers. Drastic action was needed.

The Women's Land Army (WLA) had been established during the First World War. Now it was needed again. At first the workers were volunteers, but the 1941 National Service Act permitted the conscription of single women and widows without children into the armed forces or to work in farming or industry. At first only those between twenty and thirty were involved, but later there was expansion to include women between nineteen and forty-three. Those working on farms became known as 'Land Girls'. Lady Gertrude Denman became the honorary director of the re-formed WLA and thirteen War Agricultural Committees were established in Essex, especially involved in recruitment. Mrs RE Solly-Flood became the county secretary with headquarters established at the Writtle Institute of

Agriculture. At the beginning of the war Essex had approximately 124 women working as tractor drivers, milkmaids, poultry carers and general farmhands, with another 160 on private farms or in training. This number rose to a peak of around 4,000. The Women's Timber Corps was reintroduced in April 1942.

Essex had as much as 70 per cent of its land given over to agriculture, so there was a desperate need for extra workers as the men went off to war. Much of the soil was heavy clay, so mechanization was introduced where possible. Some of the recruits were from the county, but there was an influx of others from around the country. Some of these had never before been away from the town in which they were born and knew nothing about livestock or the hard work involved in farming.

The new recruits came from a wide variety of backgrounds. These included those from offices, factories, shops and domestic service. Most had never before considered farm work. The campaigns for ever more recruits extolled the advantages of working in the open air and the healthy lifestyle. No mention was made of the long hours, low pay and the biting cold in winter, especially early in the morning. One

An advertising poster for the Women's Land Army. (With thanks to North Weald Airfield Museum)

requirement was that the women must be able to ride bicycles. Those joining the WLA were given a leaflet which clearly set out what was expected of the new recruit and what she would receive in return: 'Your promise to the Land Army is to give full-time service on the land while the war lasts, to work wherever in England or Wales you may be needed, to accept through the Land Army organization the job for which you are considered best suited, to stick to that job and not to leave it without the Land Army's knowledge and approval. Remember this promise and make a firm resolve that you will keep it.' This simple statement could be easily understood by anyone committing herself to joining the Land Army. In return the women were promised regular work with a guaranteed weekly wage which would leave not less than twenty-two shillings and six pence after paying for board and lodging. (Those under eighteen were only guaranteed eighteen shillings after paying for their living expenses.) There was also to be one week's holiday each year on full pay and a free half-day each week. Uniforms were free, as were necessary replacements.

The training of the new Essex Land Girls varied widely. For some it was almost non-existent but for anyone lucky enough to be sent to Writtle, near Chelmsford, it was excellent. Henry Ford's company was very important in Essex. The Henry Ford Institute of Agricultural Engineering, based at Boreham House, trained WLA members in driving and maintaining tractors, a side of farming that was to become ever more important throughout the war years and beyond. The grounds of the mansion were used for the growing of a wide variety of vegetables and fruit trees. Animals were also kept. Not everyone had the chance to be trained in advance of taking up a farming post, but as the war progressed some training farms were established. At Ravens Farm, Little Easton, they used local farmers to help with training and at Kingston's Farm in Matching 190 WLA members were trained. They learned milking, horse grooming, including work with heavy horses, looking after the farm machinery and many other skills which even included hedging and ditching.

In Dee Gordon's fascinating book *Essex Land Girls* she gives a number of accounts of the memories of those who worked for the WLA. Some felt that the work they did on the farms was really appreciated, but others found that many looked down on them as not being in the real armed forces. Some farmers' wives became jealous of the young girls who came to work on the farms. However, these young ladies were mainly hard-working and by their efforts helped to keep the British population fed. They should have felt justly proud of their efforts at this difficult time. In March 1941 it was decided that rissoles and vegetable sausages would be mass produced and sold at a fixed price of 8d per pound.

Starting on 21 March 1941 London and the south-east of England faced devastating new raids. One 500lb bomb hit a suburban dance hall. Such venues were very popular with munitions workers, typists and soldiers on leave and there were a number of fatalities, including women. On 16 April an all-night attack took place on London with approximately 100,000 bombs being dropped. This was the heaviest raid of the war up to that time. Nowhere was safe from the threat of attack. April 19th saw another extremely heavy raid on London when it was reported that 2,300 civilians were killed. This awful event also hit Hornchurch. In Brentwood Road, close to the airfield, the entire Gill family was wiped out. This consisted of a mother and father with their seven children aged between one and eleven years. Possibly the intended target was the airfield.

A propeller blade from a Heinkel He 111, shot down in 1941 by Wing Commander Pike in Hurricane R2253. (With thanks to North Weald Airfield Museum)

The night of 11 May 1941 was a memorable one, both for Londoners and all those living on the flight path to and from the city. The drone of the bombers flying overhead will live in the memories of all who heard them. Those in the city had become used to the attacks, but no one was fully prepared for that terrible night. It was clear and moonlit, ideal for flying but sadly giving perfect conditions for a disastrous raid: 550 German planes arrived and dropped hundreds of high-explosive bombs and approximately 100,000 incendiaries. All this happened in just a few hours, leaving much of the capital in flames. Reported dead were 1,400 and many historic buildings were either damaged or destroyed. The Chamber of the House of Commons took a direct hit. The Lords' Chamber was also damaged, but could still be taken over and used by the Lower House while the Lords were able to meet in their robing room. Although St Paul's Cathedral was damaged, the great dome continued to dominate the London skyline, to many a symbol of the triumph of good over evil. Fortunately the moonlight was also ideal for the RAF pilots to take to the skies and, according to Whitehall sources, twenty-nine enemy bombers were shot down.

Elvina Savill lived in Leigh-on-Sea. She recalled a land mine falling approximately 200 yards from her house. The family did have an Anderson shelter in the garden, but it often filled with water so they moved downstairs to sleep. It was a night when incendiary bombs were being dropped so everyone was alert and ready to put out any sudden outbreaks of fire. Elvina was in bed with her younger sister, but she knew her father was watching from the front of the house while her mother went to the shed to collect a galvanized bath. Her intention was to fill it with water, ready to douse any fire that might be started by the bombs. Then disaster struck. When the bomb fell the french windows of the room where the two girls had been sleeping were blown in. Instinctively Elvina pulled the blankets over their heads, almost certainly saving them from serious injury from flying glass. At that moment the girls' mother was still in the garden but she was blown through the back door to land on the gas stove, still clutching the galvanized bath! Later they discovered that the upstairs bath was full of lumps of clay which still contained daffodil bulbs and other strange objects including a comb and a knife. Their father was bowled along the passage beside the house as slates cascaded from the roof and he was quite badly cut, as was their neighbour. It was only later that they

Air-raid wardens with an ambulance. (With thanks to Brenda Sowerby)

discovered that two people had been killed in the explosion. Such stories were commonplace in Essex during the nights of the Blitz. Later the family found an unoccupied house in their road. The doors had been blown open but no one was living there and it was in a much better state than their own home, so they moved in. They were able to pay rent for this new house until their own was once more habitable.

May 24th was the date of the Battle of the Denmark Strait. The German battleship *Bismarck* and the heavy cruiser *Prinz Eugen* were involved. For twenty years the battle cruiser HMS *Hood* had been the world's largest warship and, alongside a new battleship, HMS *Prince of Wales*, she engaged the German ships. The *Bismarck* was damaged in the ensuing battle but HMS *Hood* was hit and destroyed when her magazine exploded. She broke up and disappeared beneath the waves within two minutes. Only three of her 1,418 crew survived. Revenge came quickly, however. It had been claimed that *Bismarck* was unsinkable, but when she was discovered in the North Atlantic between Norway and Iceland the ships of the Royal Navy were ready. Every available vessel moved in, ready to attack. Some reports claimed that as many as 100 ships took part and after a lengthy chase of approximately 1,750 miles they caught their quarry. Aircraft from HMS *Ark Royal* torpedoed and crippled the German battleship, and on 27 May 1941 she was sunk by the battleships HMS *King George V* and *Rodney*. It is believed 1,300 men went down with her. From that time on battleships lost some of their importance as submarines and aircraft became increasingly effective, thus changing the face of warfare.

In Britain March 1941 saw the introduction of the Morrison air-raid shelter. This was designed by John Baker, but took the name of the Minister of Home Security, Herbert Morrison. Its official name was the Table (Morrison) Indoor Shelter and it was at first used by those without gardens suitable for an Anderson shelter. They came in kits which could be bolted together at home. They were 6ft 6in long, 4ft wide and 2ft 6in high. During the daytime they could be used as tables, but at night it was possible to sleep under them. There was a steel top and wire mesh sides, one of which could be lifted up to form a door. Strong metal supports were fixed at each corner to support the top. A raised mesh unit lifted the sleepers up from the floor. The kit arrived ready for self-assembly in over 350 parts. The Morrison shelter was not designed to withstand a direct hit, but it did give adequate protection from blast. In all over 500,000 of these shelters were made and families earning less than £350 per year were entitled to receive one free.

The Winn family, living in Prittlewell, Southend-on-Sea, had one of these shelters which dominated the dining room of their terraced house. Pamela remembered the five of them crawling through the wire opening. At that time she was eight, her sister five and their brother, Clive, two. Their mother and grandmother also joined them in the confined space. Both the girls recalled the feeling of claustrophobia as they crawled into bed. Whether or not the adults managed to get much sleep is debateable, but the children had no problems and regarded nights in the shelter as an adventure, feeling quite safe as planes droned overhead and the occasional bomb was heard as it came down nearby. On one memorable night a bomb did drop on waste ground behind the house, but it failed to explode and was later removed.

Dagenham had developed from a small village by the outbreak of war as large council estates were built by the Greater London Council. These were to house families who had previously lived in the slums of

Aerial photograph of the Ford factory at Dagenham. (With thanks to The Ford Motor Company)

London. With its docks on the banks of the Thames it was ideal for carrying out war work. Three of its tugs, *Prince*, *Princess* and *Duke*, had been involved in the Dunkirk evacuation. They belonged to the Samuel Williams Company. Another Dagenham-based firm, the Hudson Steamship Company, carried coal from the north of England to London. As a result of enemy action a number of their ships were lost. However one, the *Dagenham*, played a part in the D-Day landings.

Another firm to be based in the town was the Ford Motor Company. At the start of the war the United States was neutral and Henry Ford opposed its involvement in the conflict, but as his health declined his son, Edsel, took an increasingly important role in running the company. He did not share his father's isolationist views. At first, when the firm wanted to be involved in the war effort, the offer was declined. It was felt that the factory, built close to the Thames at Dagenham, was vulnerable to attack by German bombers. In fact around 200 bombs fell on the building during the war years, but production was never held up for long. Attitudes towards the company changed once Winston Churchill became prime minister and contracts were given to the company. Eventually the Ford Motor Company produced 390,000 tanks and trucks, 270,000 Jeeps, over 80,000 Liberators and hundreds of thousands of spare parts, gun mounts and tools. The company even had its own Home Guard Unit with around 600 men involved. Certainly this Essex-based company made an invaluable contribution to the war effort.

In a completely different field, another Essex company made its own contribution to the war effort. Eric Kirkham Cole was born in Prittlewell. Later he and his wife started making radio sets. The firm flourished and by the outbreak of war Ekco radios in their Bakelite casings had become well known throughout the country. During the war some companies believed to be vulnerable to bombing attacks were moved to other areas. The Southend Ekco factory was one of these and the headquarters moved to Buckinghamshire. They also had what was known as a shadow factory at Malmesbury, Wiltshire. Here they concentrated on the top-secret development and production of the new radar systems. This was as part of the 'Western Development Unit'. The Bakelite moulding shop remained in Southend as the equipment used was impossible to move. Within a year the empty factory was re-equipped to make wiring looms for aircraft, including the Avro Lancaster. Radar equipment was also produced by Ekco employees. This included the AI Mk. IV and AI Mk. VIII air-interception radars and the ASV Mk. II air-to-surface-vessel radar. Aircraft radios were manufactured by the firm too.

Smaller firms in Essex also played their part. W.G. Frith Co. Ltd was close to Prittlewell Station. Here tin foil was manufactured which could be used for many purposes including the making of coloured foil for sweets and chocolate-biscuit wrappers. This may not, at first, seem to have great potential for use in time of conflict. However, aluminium foil was used to jam enemy radar systems. Cut into thin strips it could be dropped from planes and became known as Glitter, Window or Chaff.

Two Chelmsford firms did notable war work. The town was an

An early photograph of Hoffmann's Chelmsford factory. (With thanks to Jim Reeve)

important centre for light engineering and the Marconi Wireless Telegraph Company had its factory in New Street. Nearby was the Hoffmann Manufacturing Company. This company had supplied the aircraft industry with essential bearings throughout both wars. With the two companies located so close together they became regular targets for the Luftwaffe. This resulted in much damage to nearby residential properties. At one time Hoffmann's was the largest employer in the town.

On the world stage the war continued with ever-increasing ferocity. France, Holland and Belgium had all fallen to the Germans and, for the first time since the coming of the Normans, invaders landed on British soil when the Channel Islands were taken. In June 1941 the Soviet Union too was facing the full force of the enemy advance. Military sources felt that, if the Red Army could hold out until winter, the German Panzers, unused to the severity of a Russian winter, would be defeated. In the meantime the enemy advance continued. By November the German army felt the full effects of the freezing temperatures in Russia. Warm clothing was seized from Russians in occupied areas.

At home rationing continued. From 2 June it was ordered that clothes displayed in shop windows must show the price and also the number of coupons required. At this point new clothing coupons had not been printed so permission was given for margarine coupons to be used instead. A 'make do and mend' culture grew up. Clothes were altered and adapted to minimize the need to buy new ones. As far as growing children were concerned special arrangements had to be made. At St Thomas' School, Brentwood Una and Ena Felton remember having their height checked and their feet measured. Una's feet were over-sized so she was granted extra coupons to help with the problem. Their neighbour, Pamela Staples, recalls her mother making the two permitted school uniform dresses for use in the summer with two inverted pleats at the front. One dress was in the wash whilst the other was in use. On one occasion Mrs Staples turned a coat inside out so that the material could be used to make other clothes. Parachute material was also used, often to make blouses or underwear.

In August 1941 5,000 Jews were rounded up in Paris prior to deportation and in early September the German secret police gave an order that all Jews over the age of six in Germany must wear a yellow six pointed Star of David on their clothing. They were also forbidden

A skirted pillbox at Walton-on-the-Naze. (F.J. Clamp)

to leave the area in which they lived without police permission. It was realized that this order would soon apply to all Jews in occupied countries. At that point no one realized the horrors that were yet to fall upon the Jewish people.

In November 1941 disaster stuck. The aircraft carrier HMS *Ark Royal* was sunk by a German U-boat. She had been the pride of the fleet and had survived a number of previous attacks, but on this occasion her luck ran out. When the torpedo struck the majority of the crew were below deck. The concussion was violent, many lights went out and the ship quickly began listing. The explosion had happened close to the bridge on the starboard side. Fortunately the destroyer HMS *Legion* was close by. She came alongside and took off most of the crew. A few stayed behind, hoping that they could be towed back to Gibraltar. This proved to be impossible. Those still on board were evacuated shortly before the ship sank. *Ark Royal*'s aircraft had destroyed more than 100 German and Italian planes during the war.

As the year drew to a close there was an event that was to change the course of the war. On 7 December the US fleet at Pearl Harbor in Hawaii was attacked by 360 Japanese carrier aircraft. Over 2,400 people lost their lives and many ships were sunk or badly damaged. An announcement from Tokyo confirmed that Japan was at war with the United States and Great Britain. The next day President Roosevelt announced that a 'state of war exists'. The neutrality of the United States of America had ended.

CHAPTER FOUR

1942
Seeing it Through

In early 1942 the conflict in the Far East expanded. On 2 January Japanese troops took Manila in the Philippines and by 11 January they had invaded Borneo and other islands in the region. Later in the month they carried out daylight bombing raids on Singapore and their troops landed in New Guinea and the Solomon Islands. The month ended with them laying siege to Singapore, which surrendered by the middle of the following month.

Such events must have seemed far removed from life in Essex, although the county continued to face its own problems. Constant bombing raids became a nightly problem. They happened in the day as well, but somehow the attacks seemed worse after dark.

In 1942 Alma Sproggs returned to Dagenham where she went back to her old school. There she discovered that they were covering work that she had already done during her evacuation. She stayed for a while but, by then, the town was suffering from increased bombing activity. One night a bomb dropped on a nearby house. Windows were shattered and bedding destroyed. Feather beds were popular at that time and one had been hit, resulting in a cloud of feathers coming through the shattered windows like a snowstorm. Two children were killed. Alma was therefore sent to her

Alma Sproggs in 2016. (F.J. Clamp)

aunt who lived in Westcliff-on-Sea. At first she was lonely as she did not know anyone so, being fifteen by that time, she took a job in an office. Southend-on Sea was a restricted area during the war and special permission was needed before anyone could move to the town. However, her parents were able to join their daughter as she was working there.

It was necessary for all schools to adapt to the conditions of war. Children became used to lessons being abandoned when the siren wailed. Once in the shelter, talking was not allowed. If there was the sound of bombs being dropped the children were told to crouch down until it was considered safe to move again. In some cases lessons continued in the shelters, but this was often difficult as any form of lighting was necessarily subdued. In primary schools expecting children to write in cramped conditions with books balanced on their knees was almost impossible. At St Mary's School Prittlewell someone sent in a supply of recycled green wool. At that time all the children were expected to drink a third of a pint of milk at break time. This arrived in glass bottles sealed by round, cardboard disks. Each disk had a central marked ring that could be pushed in to take a straw. These disks, once washed, could be used to wind the wool round and round. It was for this purpose that the green wool was used when the children were in the shelter. Once there was no room left for any more wool to be wound the teacher cut around the rim and the strands were kept together with another piece of wool tied tightly. The cardboard was then removed and a small, fluffy ball was left behind. Several tied together made decorations, especially for babies. Sometimes teachers led singing or group poetry recitations. Times tables were also chanted.

For older children, especially those working towards public examinations, it was necessary for lessons to continue in the shelters. At Brentwood County High School, like other senior schools across the county, every student had to make sure that she carried her gas mask and the books being worked on when the siren sounded. In time limited extra lighting was installed, but it was still inadequate for those trying to study. At Brentwood County High School the staff did attempt to continue with lessons in the shelters, but it was difficult. Two classes shared the long line of benches and their teachers had to decide whether to stand back to back in the middle of the two rows of benches to talk to their own groups, or to stand at opposite ends of the rows and hope that those in the middle would be able to hear the voice of their own teacher. It is remarkable that anyone managed to pass any examinations, but they did.

As early as September 1939 records at Pitsea Junior School show that the school was affected immediately by the war. Staff numbers were down as one teacher had married during the holiday and left and one of the men was called up for military service. The school was unable to open until October and a shift system was introduced. Children from Standard 2 upwards had classes from 8.45 am until 11.30 am. Standard 1 and the Infants attended from 12.40 pm until 2.45 pm. By November the situation had eased and a normal timetable resumed. It was later that lessons were constantly interrupted by air-raid warnings and a great deal of time was spent in the shelters. Another male member of staff left to join the forces. The school building was also used to house families on a temporary basis as they had been found to be living near some unexploded delayed-action bombs. Young people frequently joined cadet forces, often organized at school. At Billericay School there was an Army Cadet Force and also a squadron of the Air Training Corps. Most of the members belonged to the school, although not all. Some of the older cadets later served in the RAF and other services.

The flat countryside in parts of Essex meant that a number of airfields were built there during the war. Debden Airfield had been opened in 1937, but it was extended during the early years of the conflict. The main aircraft flying from the airfield at that time were Hurricanes. Then, in 1941, Royal Canadian Air Force men arrived and were based at the airfield. However, the following year they moved to Bradwell. In May 1943 Debden became an American airbase. They flew Spitfires before moving on to P-47s. Bradwell Bay Airfield was less well known than many others. Work on radar took place there early in the war and this was top secret. Bradwell is a fascinating area. A Roman fort once stood on the banks of the River Blackwater and after it fell into ruin some of the bricks were used to build the church of St Peter on the Wall in AD 654, one of the oldest surviving churches in the country. There had been an airfield there before the war. Once 488 Canadian Squadron arrived they flew Douglas Boston Bombers from the base. Also in 1942 23 Squadron RAF arrived and brought with them

The wedding of Molly and George Dando at St Mary's Church, Prittlewell.
(With thanks to Brenda Sowerby)

de Havilland Mosquitoes. Other squadrons also spent time at Bradwell before the coming of 488 New Zealand Squadron.

In January 1942 the Nazis formulated a plan to establish special camps to deal with the Jews in Europe. This became known as the 'Final Solution'. It was estimated that there were 11,000,000 Jews on the continent at that time, although it was believed that thousands had already been killed. Reinhard Heydrich, right-hand man of the SS chief Heinrich Himmler, was responsible for this idea. Some claimed Heydrich's anti-Semitism was caused by rumours that his mother was half-Jewish. With Hitler's hatred of all Jews he apparently wanted to prove that he had no sympathy for them.

We have already seen that clothes rationing was causing problems. Sarah Cutter had two sewing machines, both made by the Singer Sewing Machine Company. One was a treadle and the other a hand machine. Needles could be changed to deal with different fabrics. The former was older, but they both worked well and she loved making clothes for her growing grandchildren. Men were encouraged to abandon turn-ups on trousers and women were expected to wear slightly shorter skirts. Both these recommendations were to ensure that less material was used.

The radio was of vital importance to almost every family. News programmes were listened to with avid interest, but programmes like *ITMA* (*It's That Man Again*) brought a smile to the faces of thousands. Music too cheered the nation with singers like Gracie Fields and Vera Lynn becoming household names.

By 1942 Alan Parish was once again evacuated, this time to Sudbury in Suffolk. He was six years old. He has no memory of attending school there, possibly because his arrival was close to the end of the school year. He does recall the nearby American airbase and discovered that the airmen were extremely generous and kind to the young evacuees. In the autumn he returned once more to Barking.

A history of Essex in the Second World War must include the illustrious Essex Regiment. This was a line infantry regiment formed in 1881 from the 44th (East Essex) and the 56th (West Essex) Regiments of foot. They became the 1st and 2nd Battalions of the newly formed regiment. Later the East and West Essex Regiments of Militia joined the Essex Regiment as the 3rd and 4th Battalions. There were also volunteer battalions based at Brentwood, Colchester, West

In constant use by Sarah Cutter during the war, here Emma Clamp is learning to use her great-great grandmother's sewing machine. (With thanks to David Clamp)

Ham and Walthamstow. The Regiment made notable contributions in the Second World War. The 2nd Battalion moved to France in September 1939 and was involved in the retreat from Dunkirk and later as part of the D-Day landings. The 1/4th (TA) served in North Africa, Greece and Italy, fighting at El Alamein and in the final battles leading to the surrender of the Axis forces in Africa. The Battle of Monte Cassino is still remembered for the part it played in the war, and members of the Essex Regiment were involved in this battle too. Later, during some of the most bitter fighting of the Italian campaign, the 1/5th Essex (TA) took part, as they did in the final conflict in north-west Germany. Although the 2/5th Essex was unsuccessful at Deir-El-Shein in 1942 they caused a delay to Rommel's Afrika Korps. This gave the Eighth Army time to withdraw, reorganize and make a stand on the Alamein Line.

The Regimental Chapel of The Royal Anglian Regiment and the Essex Regiment at Warley. (F.J. Clamp)

It was on 26 January 1942 that the first troops of the United States Army landed on European soil. Their landing point was in Northern Ireland. The entire operation was kept secret. The band of the Royal Ulster Rifles was not told of their destination but the men were taken to the quayside when the first ship docked and they managed to play *The Star Spangled Banner* in welcome. The Secretary of State for Air, Sir Archibald Sinclair, flew in from London to greet the new arrivals and told them that their coming marked a new stage in the world war.

News from the Western Desert was less encouraging as Rommel's tanks moved forward against the Eighth Army, putting Benghazi under threat. The bad news continued in February when it was announced that Singapore had surrendered to the Japanese and thousands of prisoners had been taken. Back at home appeals were made by the Red Cross for comforts to be sent to prisoners of war. Brentwood County

High School decided to have a Christmas Sale to raise funds for the charity. Pupils joined in with enthusiasm. Sideshows were set up in form rooms, while outside there were to be pony rides, although in the end only one aged pony, Timmy, was obtained. He worked hard all afternoon and a considerable amount of money was raised for a very worthy cause.

In February 1942 rose-hip syrup went on sale to give children more vitamins and cod liver oil was offered free to 2,000,000 extra youngsters. Although cod liver oil and malt is still remembered by many with pleasure, plain cod liver oil is not. Parents often decided this should be given in the bath to avoid it staining clothes if the recipients decided to spit it out.

Other difficulties were being felt. To save water and the fuel needed for heating, people were expected to take fewer baths and to limit the amount of water used to just five inches. Lines were painted on baths to show the correct level and King George VI ordered for this to happen at Buckingham Palace. Where possible a second household member was urged to use the same water. A further problem was that the soap ration only allowed one bar per month. In soft-water areas care had to be taken not to let the bar fall into the hot water. In hard-water areas like London and Essex it was always difficult to get a lather, but no extra allowances were given. In April the government banned the use of embroidery on women's underwear and nightwear. Presumably this was on new clothing sold in shops. Many needlewomen would happily have done their own embroidery at home.

There were other problems in the home. Shaving soap, although unrationed, was difficult to obtain. Razor blades were also in short supply and it was recommended that blunt ones could be re-sharpened by running them around the inside of a glass tumbler. As new tumblers were almost impossible to obtain only pre-war ones could be used. There was a shortage too of cosmetics. Most Essex gardens by this time had vegetable plots and now the humble beetroot came into its own. Once the root vegetable was cooked its juice could be used as a substitute for lipstick. It was also discovered that soot could be used for eye makeup. Silk stockings were in very short supply, but legs could be coloured brown by making a paint with gravy browning. Friends or family members would then be called upon to pencil in the dark seams. In Britain women's fashions now included 'bare legs for patriotism'

This group photograph was taken at the wedding of George and Molly Dando. The dress was almost certainly pre-war and probably borrowed. (With thanks to Brenda Sowerby)

and in July the Vatican announced that women without stockings would be allowed into St Peter's.

Elvina Savill wanted to join the Wrens as soon as she was old enough. What she liked was the uniform with its black silk stockings and the fact that there were no brass buttons to clean. This she eventually did, although it meant leaving Essex and moving to Portsmouth. At this time maximum clothes prices were laid down by the government. A man's suit could cost no more than £4 18s 8d but those who were able to buy the cloth could still have it made up by exclusive tailors with the cost reaching as much as thirty guineas.

The German battle cruisers *Scharnhorst* and *Gneisenau* had been under surveillance by reconnaissance aircraft in the port of Brest. However, on 2 February 1942, with the heavy cruiser *Prinz Eugen*, five destroyers and thirteen motor torpedo boats, they broke out of the harbour before first light. The fleet was spotted and its presence reported in England. Frantic activity followed involving both the RAF and the Royal Navy. Under Hornchurch Sector Control six Fairey Swordfish biplane torpedo bombers of 825 Squadron prepared for take-off. Led by Lieutenant Commander Eugene Esmonde they were to have an escort of Spitfires. They prepared to attack, but were themselves attacked by Me 109s. Dogfights followed.

As the Swordfish approached the German ships they met considerable anti-aircraft fire. The lead aircraft was hit and set on fire. Bravely the gunner, Petty Officer William Clinton attempted to put out the flames with his gloved hands. Then another shell hit the plane, ripping off the lower port wing, but, although already fatally wounded and with his gunner and observer dead, Esmonde flew on in an effort to destroy *Scharnhorst*. His plane then plunged into the sea. The other five Swordfish met a similar fate. Only five of the eighteen men were rescued. Their efforts

Molly Dando in uniform. (With thanks to Brenda Sowerby)

had been in vain. The torpedoes missed their targets and the ships reached the River Elbe. *Scharnhorst* was damaged by mines on the way, but she still managed to limp home. Although the efforts of the Hornchurch Sector were unsuccessful on that occasion all three of the major German ships involved did not survive the war unscathed. *Scharnhorst* was sunk by the Royal Navy as she prepared to attack a convoy bound for Russia on 26 December 1943. Of the 1,800 men on board only thirty-six survived. *Prinz Eugen* was attacked by a British submarine and had her stern blown off and *Gneisenau* was so badly damaged by RAF bombers while she was in dock that she took no further part in the war. Eugene Esmonde's body was washed up on the Kent coast two months later. He was awarded a posthumous Victoria Cross.

Douglas Bostons had arrived from the USA in the summer of 1941, but they could not be used with Blenheims for daylight raids until

A six-sided pillbox at Ford End. (F.J. Clamp)

February 1942. The arrival of American airmen in Essex was greeted with enthusiasm by many young ladies of the county. With so many young men serving overseas these newcomers made weekly dances far more enjoyable. In August the Hornchurch Wing formed an escort for the B-17 Flying Fortresses when these planes of the United States Eighth Air Force made their first raid over enemy-occupied territory. Fortunately the mission was successful and there were no casualties among those flying the bombers and fighters. Later there were a number of losses when the Americans ventured into Germany for daylight raids. 1942 was a bad time for Hornchurch airmen. By the end of September 345 pilots had been lost and a number were buried in the war graves area of St Andrew's, the 'horned church'.

In March the government announced the introduction of fuel rationing. The majority of houses had open coal fires and much cooking was still done in coal-fuelled ovens. At least the rationing was starting in spring, but when winter approached it would cause considerable hardship. At the end of the month the Nazis began deporting Jews to Poland where they were sent to the Auschwitz concentration camp. This was also the time when more than 200 Bomber Command aircraft launched a terrifying raid on the Baltic port of Lübeck. It was a fine, moonlit night. The town was a shipbuilding, industrial and cultural centre. Within half an hour hundreds of tons of incendiaries and high explosives had been dropped, making it almost impossible for firefighters to deal with the carnage. It was later reported that 301 people died, three were missing and 783 injured. More than 15,000 lost their homes. The RAF then began a major attack on German-controlled factories in France. They also moved on to bomb towns and factories in the Ruhr Valley. Inevitably this action resulted in retaliation. Hitler ordered the Luftwaffe to make increased attacks on British targets, attacks that would have a disastrous impact on the civilian population. He decided that every British town listed in the Baedeker guidebook should be razed to the ground. Exeter, Bath, Norwich and York were all targeted. Every county in the country must have feared that their cities would be next. Overseas, the Soviets held back further German advances, but Japan continued its aggression. The Japanese captured Bataan in the Philippines and took many prisoners. The Allies bombed the main Burmese oil fields to stop them falling into Japanese hands. In May Japan took Mandalay, in Burma.

On 19 July at around 6.15 am a single German Dornier Do 217 flew low over the Hoffmann ball-bearing factory in Chelmsford. It came in with machine guns blazing and dropped four 500kg high-explosive bombs before escaping. Three of the bombs hit the factory while the fourth fell on residential properties in Rectory Lane. Four men died in the factory, Charles Brett, James Brennan, Daniel Gannon and Patrick Moffatt. Charles Brett was forty years old and he lived with his wife and three children in Wickford.

In October the two major factories of Marconi and Hoffmann were again targets for a bombing raid. On this occasion a bomb aimed at Hoffmann's bearings factory hit the roof but ricocheted off. It passed through one house but exploded close to the home of Denis Locke in Henry Road. His mother died as did four others as a result of this raid. Denis was an invalid. He was found to have been blown out of the house, still in bed. He was taken to Black Notley County Sanatorium

The RAF memorial stained-glass window at North Weald. This was unveiled by Lord Tebbit, a former RAF pilot at North Weald. (With thanks to North Weald Airfield Museum)

where he died later in the month. The raid resulted in five houses being completely demolished and another nine damaged beyond repair. Many others were also damaged. Again the attack had involved a single Dornier Do 217E flying low over the town.

Southend also suffered a number of bombing raids in 1942. As early as 9 January HMS *Vimiera* had struck a mine in the Thames Estuary. In July acoustic mines were dropped in the Estuary, but it was on 10 October that there was serious bombing in the High Street. The London Hotel, R.A. Jones, the well-known jewellers, and the Cash Clothing Store were all hit. A single Messerschmitt Bf 109 flew over the sea front on the same day, shooting at civilians in the area. The death toll reached four and a further forty-six were injured. Later in the month a Bf 110 managed to enter the Estuary and then turned towards Southend High Street. Bombs were dropped and there was machine-gun fire. A number of well-known local men were killed including the Cash Clothing Store manager. The poor man had escaped the bombing of his shop earlier in the month, but this time he was less fortunate.

Hitler's oppression of the Jews continued unabated. At the end of June every Jewish school in Germany was closed. Life for members of this persecuted religion was becoming ever more difficult. There was also horrifying news from Poland that more than 700,000 had been murdered and in Romania at least 125,000 were dead. In Holland, Belgium and France daily executions were taking place. In Libya and beyond Rommel continued to make progress. The Eighth Army fought bravely, but they were being forced back. It was also in June that Major-General Dwight D. Eisenhower was given command of all the United States forces in Europe. As a result of this appointment many believed that there would soon be an Allied landing in Europe.

East Anglia, with its flat countryside, was ideal for air fields. Boxstead Airbase was developed in the summer of 1942 and was given over to the Eighth Air Force. It was used by B-26s for bombing raids. The following year the Ninth Air Force used it as a fighter base flying P-51B Mustangs. This plane was unsatisfactory until the engines were replaced by Rolls-Royce Merlins. Later in the war the 5th Emergency Rescue Group was formed. Their P-47s were converted from carrying bombs to carrying dinghies. These were dropped into the water to rescue pilots who had come down in the North Sea.

1942 was an eventful year for those living in Frinton and Walton

EASTERN REGIONAL TRAINING SCHOOL
INTER - SERVICE COURSE   Nº II   19-10-42

The Eastern Regional Training School, 1942. (With thanks to Brenda Sowerby)

Urban District. The lifeboats from Walton and Clacton were in constant demand. In mid-February the Clacton lifeboat was alerted when a Wellington bomber came down near the shore. Sadly five died, but two were saved. Bombs and mines were frequently washed ashore and all had to be investigated. Frinton had become the home of 45th Division's Battle School with the officers' mess being located in the golf clubhouse. The end of the course saw manoeuvres frequently carried out on the Naze cliffs. These training exercises were as realistic as possible and the climb up the unstable cliffs must have been terrifying. On 26 August four high-explosive bombs were dropped at the Naze. Three exploded, causing considerable damage to property, and there were three minor casualties. The tennis court pavilion took a direct hit and a nearby house was damaged beyond repair.

Properties close to the coast were especially vulnerable. On 10 October a Dornier Do 215 dropped three or four bombs into the sea close to Frinton. The enemy plane escaped but twelve properties were found to have minor damage following the explosions. On 10 November six more seafront properties at Frinton suffered minor damage as a result of practice gunfire by coastal defence batteries.

As the towns of north-east Essex dealt with their own problems the war continued to gain momentum. In June, after four days of fierce fighting in the Pacific Ocean around Midway Island, the Japanese navy was forced to withdraw. Attacks had occurred by both sea and air. The Japanese losses were severe, four of their six fleet aircraft carriers being lost, while the American destroyer *Hammon* was sunk by a submarine and the aircraft carrier *Yorktown* was abandoned after being hit. In the desert, with the Eighth Army unable to respond, Rommel's troops moved forward towards Cairo. Previously Tobruk had been lost by the Allies and many prisoners were taken by the enemy. However, better news came in July. The Eighth Army, after a fierce battle, held the line at El Alamein. Rommel's advance was halted. The same month there was encouraging news when it was learned that the United States Air

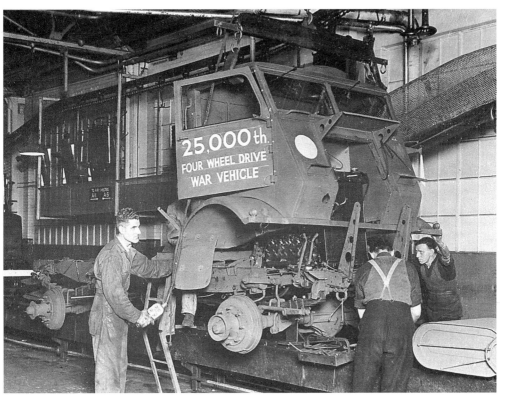

A Ford worker with a four-wheel drive vehicle. (With thanks to The Ford Motor Company)

Force, flying planes from British bases, had bombed German air bases in Holland. There were accounts of the bombing of U-boat yards in Danzig by Lancaster bombers. The RAF also carried out its first daylight bombing of the Ruhr industrial area. For the children of Essex and throughout the country there was the devastating news that sweet rationing was to be introduced. With sugar being in short supply it is hardly surprising that this became necessary, if unpopular.

1942 saw some changes in the Women's Land Army. Many Land Girls had never been away from home before and it could be a lonely experience. Often up to half their weekly wage disappeared to pay for food and lodging. Yet as conscription was extended more young women joined the numbers working on the land. Hostels were needed to accommodate this influx and some used requisitioned property, whilst others were purpose-built. Cranham saw the first Land Girls' settlement and this was even visited by R.S Hudson, the Minister of Agriculture. Around twenty young women lived there, the majority coming from large towns. They were described in the local paper as being happy and contented. At least in this type of accommodation they were able to discuss with others in the same situation any problems that might arise. An April 1942 report in *The Land Girl*, the official magazine of the service, said that there were eight barrack hostels, one hutment and eight house hostels in Essex. One large hostel was in Thundersley, not far from St Peter's church. Another was in Mark Hall, Harlow, an impressive house with very large rooms. The young ladies were expected to be home by 10 pm unless they had a special late pass. Land Girls often moved from one billet to another and there were many across the county. The hostels had a warden or supervisor to watch over the young land workers. Some had strict rules, but others were more relaxed.

As the summer progressed a new heavy bomber, the Avro Lancaster, came off the secret list. This had a range of 3,000 miles, could fly at 300mph, carried a bomb load of eight tons and was armed with eight machine guns. The head of Bomber Command, Air Marshal Sir Arthur Harris, threatened Germany with virtually non-stop bombing by the RAF and the United States Air Force. Lancaster squadrons had already made the longest daylight bombing attack of the war when Danzig was targeted. The planes were constructed in underground factories in Britain and also in Canada. They soon became essential for the night bombing campaign.

A Lancaster bomber. (With thanks to The Norfolk RAF Air Defence Radar Museum)

Frank Dudley was seventeen when he left Southend and joined the RAF. He did various courses in England but was then sent to South Africa where he qualified as a navigator and returned to England to work on Lancaster bombers. He recalled his time as a navigator and the little cabin where he worked. It had a black curtain that could be pulled round to stop any light from escaping. They used highly sophisticated instruments called G Sets. Much to his surprise he found the name and address of E.K. Cole printed on them – not the best idea in time of war!

In August General Bernard Montgomery became commander of the Eighth Army. He was a firm believer in Spartan training methods and on one occasion organized a ten-day endurance test with the men surviving on iron rations. In October, under their new commander, the Eighth Army launched a major offensive along the coast at El Alamein. Then, at the end of the month, General Montgomery gave the order and one thousand guns roared into action. This was the start of the Battle of El Alamein. At this time the Axis forces were under the command of General Stumme as Rommel was in a German

General Montgomery visiting Warley Barracks. (With thanks to Sylvia Kent)

sanatorium. Stumme was on the way to his command post when his car came under fire. He suffered from high blood pressure and died of a heart attack. Rommel rushed back, but was too late to stop the Allied advance. This was a great victory and church bells rang for the first time since 1940 when the German invasion was feared. If this had happened the bells would have been used as a warning.

Early in September 1942 it was reported that SS troops had cleared the Jewish ghetto in Warsaw, killing approximately 50,000 people. Many were executed and others sent to concentration camps. The walled ghetto was destroyed with the use of flamethrowers and grenades. Some died jumping from roofs or were burned in their houses. At home rationing continued to bite and the milk ration was cut to two and a half pints per week, although children still received their third of a pint each day at school. Weddings too were affected by the war. If family members had saved their pre-war dresses these were often gratefully received and altered by young brides. Parachute silk was also used. The wedding cake was limited by wartime regulations. They could no longer be iced. Instead 'cakes' could be hired from confectioners. These were made of cardboard and the 'icing' was made with chalk! Attractive perhaps, but hardly edible.

This was a time for keeping up morale. The most popular songs in 1942 were 'This is the Army Mr Jones', 'White Christmas' and 'We'll Meet Again'. These could be heard on radios throughout the country and were often sung in factories as the radio was played while people worked. Cinemas were full as people tried to escape from the realities of war. Elvina Saville recalled a visit to the Corona cinema in Leigh on Sea. One of the Bob Hope and Bing Crosby 'Road' films was featured. When the lights went up she was shocked to see that she was the only female there. The rest of the audience seemed to be a sea of khaki uniforms.

As the year drew to an end the population remembered both good and bad times. Would victory come when the New Year dawned? There were few who thought this was a realistic prospect. It was a time to accept the restrictions affecting everyday life and hope and pray that family members fighting abroad would be safe in the days to come.

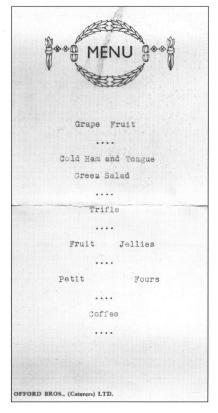

The menu for Molly and George Dando's wedding in 1942. (With thanks to Brenda Sowerby)

CHAPTER FIVE

1943

Turning the Corner

1943 started well for the Allies. On 1 January the Japanese began withdrawing from Guadalcanal in the Solomon Islands. By the 10th of the month the United States had started a major offensive there, and by early in February all resistance on the island appeared to have ceased. It was announced in Tokyo that Japanese forces had been withdrawn from both Guadalcanal and New Guinea. The airstrip at Guadalcanal would be extremely useful to the Americans as it was within range of the Japanese base at Rabaul.

At the beginning of January the Soviet army claimed to have captured the German base at Chernyevskaya. This was important for both rail and air facilities. Another success came for General Leclerc's Free French troops when they took Oum-el-Araneb, the main Axis base in south Libya. Later in the month these troops merged with the Eighth Army under the command of General Montgomery.

Not all the news was good in Essex, where air raids continued. Occasionally harm was caused by friendly fire, as when on 4 January a house in Hall Lane, Walton, was damaged by anti-aircraft gunfire. Two days later an enemy aircraft machine-gunned houses in Kirby Road, Kirby-le-Soken. Damage to property was also caused by the explosion of landmines buried in the unstable cliffs.

On 28 January *Resolute*, a wheat-carrying barge from Mistley, struck a mine not far from Holland Haven. The Clacton lifeboat was launched in eight minutes. The speed involved in this launch was achieved because the lifeboat men did not wait for a full crew. The skipper of *Resolute* was rescued by another barge and then transferred to the Clacton boat.

Nurses in outdoor uniform. (With thanks to Brenda Sowerby)

Walton-on the Naze had a very active war. The Naze itself was taken over by the military and, as we have seen, it formed part of the Essex coastal defences, which included barbed-wire lining the beaches, minefields and pillboxes. The latter were often disguised as beach huts or other seaside attractions. They were also to be found on the cliff top. When the unstable cliffs shifted they were liable to cause mines to explode. There were similar defences at other nearby seaside towns including Frinton, Holland-on-Sea and Clacton.

Two sea forts were built near Walton. One was named Rough Tower and the other Sunk Head. They were armed with two 3.7in anti-aircraft guns and two Bofors guns. After the war the forts were abandoned. Keith Hall of Southend remembers barbed wire and large concrete blocks lining the seafront. As in other seaside towns this was protection in case of invasion. There was no access to the beach for anyone without official authority, which was frustrating for local children.

Internationally there were more successes. At the end of January 1943 Mosquito bombers were sent on two daylight raids on Berlin. At the time Reichsmarshall Hermann Göring was about to make a broadcast celebrating the fact that the Nazi regime had been in existence for ten years. Many Germans were already tuned to their radios and so were unprepared for a daytime attack. Hardly any flak was encountered by the British pilots. Both attacks were successful. Allied troops also captured Tripoli. This was the last city held by Mussolini in Africa. Montgomery received the surrender.

In 1943 there was still some prejudice against women workers, many of whom had never before been involved in agricultural work. In July 1941 the *Essex Chronicle* had reported that most Land Girls were excellent workers, especially those involved with market gardening and poultry work. However, in January 1943 the same paper pointed out that many recruits still lacked adequate training. The Waltham Abbey branch of the National Farmers' Union resolved that all Land Girls should receive some training before being sent to farms. One member pointed out that no ATS recruit would be expected to carry out specialized war work without adequate training, but another member stated that the best place for them to learn was on the farm.

A case of colour prejudice even hit the national headlines. Amelia King came from Stepney and was of Afro-Caribbean descent. Her father and brother were both serving in the Navy. Amelia applied to the Women's Land Army, only to hear that she had been turned down by the Essex County Committee. No reason was given and instead she was told she could do munitions work. She later discovered that the reason for her rejection was her colour. Unwilling to accept this decision she took her case to Parliament. Eventually her fight was successful and she was accepted by the WLA.

By March there were constant air raids on the Ruhr, the heartland of Germany's industry. A report to the House of Commons stated that around 2,000 factories had been destroyed or badly damaged with the loss of the production of many tons of steel. Coal extraction was down by 20 per cent. Essen had been badly hit and had lost at least thirty engineering shops. Berlin was also hit by high explosives and incendiary bombs. Goebbels admitted to the newspapers that there had been severe bombing, but it was not affecting the war effort.

No account of the devastation in the Ruhr Valley can be complete without a mention of the effects of the 'Dambusters' raid. This was later immortalized in the extremely popular film of that name with its memorable theme tune. What is not always realized is that an Essex establishment played its own important role in the operation. Planning started long before the actual raid in May 1943. Specially-adapted Lancaster bombers were to be used in the attack. These were capable of flying low. The attack was to be made by night and the aim was to destroy the dams. Water from the reservoirs behind the dams would then flood down onto the factories below, destroying them completely. Dr Barnes Wallis was the brains behind the development of the unique Bouncing Bomb and 617 Squadron was chosen to make the attack under the leadership of Wing-Commander Guy Gibson.

At that time the Royal Gunpowder Mills at Waltham Abbey were important for the production of cordite and early in the war they were the sole producers of ADX, a component of Torpex, the explosive used in the Bouncing Bomb. Once dropped the bombs skipped over the surface of the water, reached the wall and then sank to the bottom before exploding at the foot of the dam. Each bomb had to be dropped whilst being flown at exactly 220 miles per hour and with the plane precisely 60 feet above the water. Precision flying was essential. The bombs had to be dropped 425 yards from the dam wall.

The Royal Gunpowder Mills at Waltham Abbey. (F.J. Clamp)

The attack took place on 16 May when nineteen bombers left from Scampton in Lincolnshire. The main aim was to attack the Möhne, Eder and Sorpe dams. The first two were successfully breached but eight planes were lost with fifty-six men. As a result of the attack on the Möhne Dam, there was severe flooding and 1,200 people were killed, but most of the damage was short-term. The operation was used as a very successful propaganda exercise and the Waltham Abbey Gunpowder Mills had played an important part.

At home the population was still being encouraged to 'Dig for Victory'. This was something almost everyone could do, even if only on a very small scale. Essex land was fertile and some of the allotments started at that time and during the Great War are still in existence today. Vegetables and fruit were stored carefully, often by drying. Apples were sometimes cut into slices and cored. They were then hung on strings to dry and could later be reconstituted by boiling. This was long before almost every family had a freezer or even a refrigerator.

By 1943 a battery of anti-aircraft guns had been installed in Barking Park, not far from the home of Alan Parrish. Once the air-raid siren was heard the sound of exploding shells echoed around the area and the house shook. At such times the family either hid in the cupboard under the stairs or, if they were eating, under the oak dining table. Following such raids boys would search the area for bomb fragments or shrapnel.

One very notable Essex fighter base was at North Weald. It had been founded in 1916 by the Royal Flying Corps and it continued to grow in the inter-war years. Large hangers and accommodation for service personnel were built. When war broke out again it was used, at first as a base for Hawker Hurricanes and Bristol Blenheims which were used as night fighters. Hurricanes flew over Dunkirk giving support as the Allies left the beaches and the planes also played an important part in the Battle of Britain. Spitfires were used by two American Eagle Squadrons who moved to North Weald and later Norwegian squadrons arrived. After the end of the war the airfield continued to be used by the RAF until they finally withdrew in 1969. North Weald is still an active airport and it has an excellent museum housing reminders of the role played by its airmen during both World Wars. A replica of a Hawker Hurricane Mk 1 can be seen close to the main gate.

Construction of the airfield at Stanstead began in 1942. It was built

RAF uniform. (With thanks to North Weald Airfield Museum)

by the Americans and in 1943 became one of the first bases for the United States Army Air Force (USAAF). For a while it served as a service depot until a bomb group arrived. They flew B-26 Marauder bombers, but these were left unpainted and so became known as Silver Streaks. By the end of the war it became a storage base and a rest centre for airmen returning from Europe. After the RAF took over Stanstead it was used for a time as a prisoner-of war-camp. American airmen were posted to many Essex airfields, often flying for fighter groups or bomber squadrons. They were based at Andrews Field near Braintree, previously known as Great Saling, Birch near Colchester, Boreham, four miles from Chelmsford, Chipping Ongar and many other airfields throughout the county. Stanstead, now a major airport, would be unrecognizable to those who made it their base during the war. Other once busy airfields have reverted to farming or leisure activities.

By 1943 it was realized that the threat of invasion had diminished. Some of the precautions taken were now abandoned. In April Winston Churchill announced in the House of Commons that church bells could once again be rung regularly on Sundays and other special occasions. A delighted Archbishop of York was able to say that the bells of the Minster would be rung in a broadcast on Easter Day.

Unfortunately not all restrictions were eased at this time, and in some ways conditions worsened. The April budget raised the price of alcohol and put a 100 per cent tax on luxuries. Utility-designed clothes used a minimum of fabric so designs often lacked imagination, although this was not always the case. Some couture designers kept to the restrictions, but still managed to produce some very special outfits. Most utility products, including furniture, were of fairly basic design, although much welcomed by those who had lost their homes through bombing.

The CC41 Utility logo had been introduced in 1941 by the British Board of Trade. The symbol stood for Controlled Commodity and the 41 showed the year of introduction. With the number of those joining the military increasing there was an ever-growing need for uniforms for the armed forces. As a result less material was available for civilian use and shortages at home became ever more apparent. Prices rose rapidly. It was realized that some control was necessary. The number of buttons allowed on garments was limited. Suits had to be single-breasted and the height of heels was restricted.

Reproduced wartime posters decorate a café in 2016. (F.J. Clamp)

With the introduction of utility clothing manufacturers received their raw materials on a quota basis. These clothes became popular as they were tax free. Metford Watkins became Director of Civilian Clothing at the Board of Trade. It was his Directorate that had appointed Reginald Shipp to design a symbol to appear on all utility products. Some felt the two 'Cs' looked like two cheeses and might stand for Civilian Clothing.

With a severe shortage of raw materials, including wood in which Britain was not self-sufficient, utility furniture was introduced in 1942. When houses and furniture were lost through bombing there were problems. Wood was in very short supply and this caused a severe furniture shortage. The new furniture was rationed and only available to those who had been bombed out and to newly-weds. The same logo was used for furniture as for clothes. In 1943 the Utility Furniture Catalogue was published. The designs lacked the ornamentation that had been so popular in the pre-war years but they were serviceable and labour-saving. The Utility Furniture scheme finally closed in 1952. In Essex Utility clothing was worn by many, but those with needlework skills continued to alter existing garments or buy material. Singer sewing machines became prized possessions. Old woollen clothes were often unpicked and made into skeins by winding the wool around the back of a chair. This could then be steamed or washed to remove the crinkles. Pamela and Frances Winn remembered a family friend who had acquired a large supply of maroon wool. For a number of years, as the girls were growing up, she made them maroon jumpers and cardigans for Christmas. As Pamela outgrew her latest present it was passed on to Frances. Neither of them ever bought maroon clothes in later years!

By mid-April the situation for the remaining Jews in Warsaw had become desperate. In 1940 it was believed the ghetto held 300,000 Jews. Within two years only 50,000–60,000 were thought to remain. Many had died of starvation or disease while others had been 'resettled'. This meant the SS had removed them to extermination camps. Now, under General Jürgen Stroop 2,000 troops were directed into the ghetto wearing steel helmets and travelling in armoured vehicles. They carried machine guns, grenade launchers, flamethrowers and mortars. More troops were sent in, many wearing dark goggles and drab brown uniforms – a terrifying sight for children and adults alike. It had been expected that the last survivors would go quietly. They did not. They were prepared to fight to the end. As the carnage continued Jewish men, women and children retreated to the sewers, fighting as they went. The solution as far as Stroop was concerned was to flood the sewers.

As the Polish Jews faced this inhuman persecution, Holland was put under martial law as the Germans prepared for an Allied invasion. A similar fear existed in Italy where a state of emergency was declared in the south of the country and also in the Ruhr area following the 'Dambusters' raid. Italy faced a devastating Allied attack when more than 100 planes were destroyed on the ground. Towards the end of May 2,000 tons of bombs were dropped by the RAF on Dortmund. This was the heaviest raid on Germany at that time.

The cost of the war was immense and there was a desperate need for the government to raise more funds. National Saving Stamps had

More armoured vehicle tests on the Rainham marshes. (With thanks to The Ford Motor Company)

first been introduced in 1916 during the Great War and they continued until 1976. These were sold in post offices and schools and they were then stuck on a card. Lois Holmes, née Hance, well remembers being given a ten shilling note to buy stamps at her school in Leigh-on-Sea, but she lost the money. Many Essex schools were very proud of the amount they collected and there was keen competition between them.

Although the news from abroad began to give hope at home there were still many enemy bombing raids taking place. Essex remained especially vulnerable to the surplus bombs being dropped as planes returned to the Continent. It was on a Sunday afternoon early in March that the Frinton and Walton area suffered an unexpected and deadly attack. It is thought six Focke-Wulf Fw 190 fighter-bombers came in low over the two towns. First they used machine guns and then dropped six high-explosive bombs, three on Frinton, two on Walton and one on Lower Kirby. The attack happened at great speed, but the results were

A spigot mortar base at Coalhouse Fort. (F.J. Clamp)

devastating. Six were killed and fourteen injured and a number of properties were damaged or destroyed. Kirby had two houses damaged in the attack, but Frinton and Walton had more serious problems.

One of the high-explosive bombs landing at Frinton fell close to the railway crossing. There were a number of injuries but none too serious. A second 250kg bomb failed to explode. It fell on a house and ended up in the living room. The third destroyed an empty house. However, two nearby houses were badly damaged. They were being used as billets for members of the 2/7th Royal Warwickshire Regiment. Sadly two nineteen-year-old soldiers were killed and a third injured by shrapnel. The regiment was only in the town for a brief stay and moved away just a fortnight later.

Two bombs hit Walton, falling fairly close together. Four cottages and a shop were destroyed. Four lives were lost and there were several injuries. It is believed that the bomb that caused the damage landed first in a coal yard close to the railway but bounced off a crane and then carried on to the unfortunate cottages. Nine people in the town were left homeless after the raid and they were temporally placed in the Congregational Church Hall Rest Centre, and 150 others were evacuated while an unexploded bomb in Green Way was defused.

Another Sunday attack was made on Frinton and Walton at the end of May. This was in the evening and was again made by Focke-Wulf Fw 190 fighter-bombers. (The exact number involved is not certain, but it is thought there may have been as many as twenty.) They approached at speed from the south, coming in over the sea before turning to approach the towns from the landward side. The planes flew in so low that many of the bombs failed to explode on initial impact, instead bouncing back up to explode when they fell a second time. The raid took approximately one minute, but in that time at least twenty high-explosive bombs fell. Because of the way in which the planes had approached no air-raid warning had sounded so there was no time for civilians to reach shelter.

A V8 engine at Fords' Dagenham plant. (With thanks to The Ford Motor Company)

Seven more bombs fell in Frinton, one on The Esplanade, cutting the road in half. Another fell outside the Grand Hotel, causing considerable damage. Two churches, St Mary's and the Free Church, both had broken windows, although no one was reported as being injured. As a service was going on in the Free Church at the time many of those present must have suffered from severe shock. Three other bombs fell in Third Avenue. A Civil Defence ambulance driver died of his injuries after the Civil Defence Rescue Depot Offices were hit by a ricocheting bomb. The final Frinton bomb hit the water tower by the railway line but bounced off to land between two bungalows. One of the buildings was demolished and the other badly damaged, but the occupants were saved by being in their Morrison shelter, although they suffered some non-life-threatening injuries. Apparently two of the enemy planes, after dropping their loads, headed out to sea and collided. One crashed into the water.

One bomb fell on farmland between the two towns so did little damage, but five fell on Walton. The first failed to explode but nearby residents were forced to leave their homes while it was de-activated. Another landed near the cemetery and a third made a direct hit on the home of the Smith family. Mrs Smith and her two daughters were killed. Mr Smith was in the garden at the time and was badly injured. A direct hit destroyed the Roman Catholic Church on the corner of Martello Road and the police station was too badly damaged to be used for the rest of the war. The home of Major and Mrs Cripps was also hit. Mrs Cripps died, but her husband, who was also in the garden, survived. Although here we have looked at two towns suffering during 1943 others throughout Essex were under attack as well, especially from planes dropping leftover bombs before returning home. Daily there were new attacks and no one could ever feel completely safe. The fear of invasion might have receded, but the threat of attack from the skies was ever-present.

With so many men involved in the war there was a need for ever more women to enter employment. In early May the government, led by the Labour Minister Ernest Bevin, decided that women aged between eighteen and forty-five should do compulsory part-time war work. Those with domestic responsibilities were excluded. Part-time meant up to thirty hours each week. There was a special need for workers in shops and factories. During a specified period managers

The tower at Walton-on-the-Naze. A radar aerial was added later in the war. (F.J. Clamp)

were not allowed to sack these women, but the workers were not permitted to leave their employment except in exceptional circumstances and absenteeism was regarded as an offence.

It was in 1943 that the number of ships sunk by U-boats began to decline. During 1942 approximately 650,000 tons of Allied shipping had been lost each month. In April 1943 this had dropped to 245,000 tons and in May it had fallen to 18,000. Seventeen U-boats had been sunk. Successes in North Africa had led to more escort ships and aircraft carriers becoming available to hunt U-boats in the Atlantic where most of the damage had been done. Radar had also progressed and Asdic sets, using sound waves, helped to detect submarines under water. Other scientific advances were also helping the Allied cause.

Sydney Bridge was living in Southend, but when the war started his father was advised to move to Dorset for health reasons. Sydney and his wife had a three-month-old baby at that time and it was decided that the young mother and her son should go with them as it would probably be safer than Southend. At that time he was working for the Southend Libraries Department. Then a request came to the local authority asking for volunteers with office experience to join the Royal Army Ordinance Corps. Sydney joined up, but found the work rather boring. Then he saw an advertisement for volunteers to join the Intelligence Corps. This sounded interesting but applicants needed to speak a foreign language, other than French. The last time he had used German was at school but he applied, did a test and was accepted. His first posting was to the Lake District but then he was ordered to go overseas. Much to his surprise, when his ship moored for the first night, he discovered that they were just off Southend Pier, which was in constant use for the transfer of men and supplies. This was a brief and unexpected homecoming.

From 1942 onward American air force and army personnel were arriving in Britain, especially in East Anglia. Many of the RAF airfields were also used by the USAAF. By 1943 there were over 100,000 US servicemen in the United Kingdom with many of them based in Essex, including the Eighth and some of the Ninth Air Force. The arrival of these friendly allies made a big difference to life in Essex. This was the time of the big bands and local ladies attended dances with enthusiasm. They learnt to jitterbug and were introduced to luxuries like peanut butter, chewing gum, coca cola and nylons.

The American Red Cross Service Club at the Saracen's Head Hotel, Chelmsford. (With thanks to Jim Reeve)

The pier at Southend-on-Sea, renamed HMS Leigh *during the war. (F.J. Clamp)*

On a more serious note the USAAF arrived with the B-17 Flying Fortress and the B-24 Liberator heavy bombers and the P-51 Mustang fighter. They also used the P-38 Lightning and the P-47 Thunderbolt fighters. Hornchurch aircraft acted as escorts for the Flying Fortresses when they set off for the Continent. Some of these flights were highly successful, but others were not. In all 30,000 American airmen were lost flying from the UK during the war. The escorting planes had a limited range and had to leave the Fortresses and Liberators over Belgium. Later this problem was solved for the Americans when the P-51s were fitted with supplementary fuel tanks under their wings, thus increasing their range.

The 'Make Do and Mend' culture continued in Essex and many sewing machines were used to alter and re-use material from other garments, many dating from pre-war days. The Board of Trade claimed that £600 million had been saved as a result of clothes rationing. Apparently the average family of four each year spent £20 per head before the war. This had now been reduced to just £7.10s. By adapting old clothes it was possible to personalize clothing and make more adventurous garments than those offered in shops. At the end of May it was announced that signposts could once more be erected in rural areas. These had been removed when the fear of invasion was at its height.

Although the general public still lived with the knowledge that they could be bombed at any time, the government was making plans for a victorious and peaceful future. In July ideas were unveiled for a ring road around London. A White Paper also recommended that, in the post-war period, all children should have free education until the age of sixteen. No one realized how long it would take for these plans to be realized.

Most Essex towns still have maps of where bombs fell during the war. In Brentwood there were 43 killed and 432 wounded. The bombs were of different types; high explosive, incendiary, V-1 Doodlebugs and V-2 rockets. Fortunately a number failed to explode and others missed buildings and landed instead in fields and woodland.

As the summer progressed the Allies recorded an increasing number of successes. In July, the greatest tank battle in history took place around Kursk, to the south of Moscow. When Hitler's troops attacked the Soviets were fully prepared and eventually the Germans were

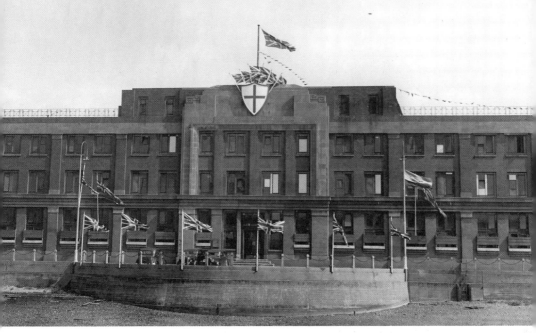

Fords' of Dagenham. (With thanks to The Ford Motor Company)

forced back. On 23 July the Sicilian capital of Palermo fell to the Americans. This victory neutralized one of the main Axis submarine bases in the Mediterranean and also gave the Allies a new airfield from which strikes could be made on German and Italian positions, well behind their lines. It was in late July that Mussolini, the Fascist dictator of Italy, was deposed by King Victor Emmanuel after twenty-one years in power. Early in August RAF bombers attacked Hamburg by night and the United States Air Force attacked by day. 10,000 tons of bombs were dropped on the city over a period of eight days. Much of Hamburg was destroyed in the onslaught, including factories and shipyards. Civilian casualties were known to be extremely high. Early in September Eisenhower announced that Italy had surrendered to the Allies. The Nazis were taken by surprise. Just one hour earlier Berlin radio had reported that there was 'solid resistance' from the German and Italian forces to the British invasion of southern Italy. Meanwhile Mussolini had been spirited away from Italy by the Germans.

Successes might have be recorded on mainland Europe but Walton and Frinton continued to face constant attacks. Fw 190 fighter-bombers still made regular flights over the area in what were known as 'tip and run' raids. On the evening of 6 September a Mosquito aircraft was patrolling over the Channel when information came in of an enemy

The Guy Gibson display. (With thanks to Canvey Bay Museum)

plane approaching from the south. The intruder was traced and both planes crossed the coast near Clacton. Searchlights picked out the enemy aircraft but then they both entered cloud. The German plane dropped its load close to Ipswich. Squadron Leader Howitt then moved in on the Fw 190 and fired. The enemy plane was hit and plunged vertically towards the sea. It was later reported that Unteroffizier Helmut Breier had failed to return following a mission on 6 September. Almost certainly he was the pilot concerned with the raid.

Since May U-boats had been fairly quiet in the Atlantic, but in late September and early October they became active once more and several ships were sunk. On a brighter note Winston Churchill announced in November that 700 U-boats had been destroyed since the start of the war including sixty over the previous three months. After surrendering to the Allies the Italian government changed sides, much to the consternation of the Nazis. As the Germans retreated from the country they left devastation behind. There were reports of Rome being looted and food stocks destroyed. The Soviets continued to have successes. In late October 1943 the Red Army unexpectedly crossed the River Dnieper to break through the German lines. Knowing that the bridges were unusable they adapted a variety of craft for their crossing including small rowing boats, improvised rafts, planks and even garden benches. The Nazis were unprepared for the Russian attack but they still managed to hold the Crimea, which had useful airfields.

Una and Ena Felton of Brentwood were not evacuated but they did have evacuees from London. Their father was born in 1891, so he was too old for war work but he was a coalman and would sometimes return home with a rabbit or chicken supplied by a grateful customer. He was also an air-raid warden and he put a book on his front door which was signed by the other wardens when they came on and off duty. As a warden he also visited the Ursuline Convent where the nuns liked to give the wardens a much-appreciated hot drink. If it was raining they would be able to dry their gloves and socks. The family, like many others, had a bucket of water on the doorstep in case incendiary bombs were dropped.

The radar tower at Coalhouse Fort, built to report enemy ships coming up the Thames. (F.J. Clamp)

Bombing was still a constant fear. On one occasion a bomb dropped where the multi-storey car park now stands and a landmine fell on the Congregational School Rooms in Crown Street, Brentwood, completely destroying them. Mr Felton had his lorry filled with coal at the railway station. One day he watched as a plane dropped a bomb so he sheltered under a railway truck. The bomb fell nearby in Myrtle Road, close to the railway, which was probably the intended target, but he was safe.

It was in early December 1943 that Ernest Bevin, the Minister of Labour, announced that one in ten men called up between the ages of eighteen and twenty-five would be sent to work in the coal mines. There was an acute shortage of manpower in the mines as many young miners had enlisted earlier to get away from the work and conditions involved. The conscripts were to be chosen by ballot, so there was a complete mixture of social classes. They were quickly dubbed 'Bevin Boys'.

Berlin faced heavy bombing by the RAF. More than 12,000 tons of high explosives were dropped by 1,000 bombers. Plans were made to evacuate the city but, at the same time, the German propaganda machine threatened retaliation against Britain by using a secret weapon. All too soon the British people were to discover the nature of that weapon.

As Christmas approached the government announced that there would only be enough turkeys for one family in ten, but the civilian population tried to remain cheerful. Many houses were decorated with homemade paper chains and any other adornments that had been saved from the pre-war years. There was optimism that the Allies would be victorious before too long. Unfortunately there were still more horrors to be faced before such dreams became reality.

CHAPTER SIX

1944

Hitting Back

At the start of 1944 the population felt a mixture of hope and despair. Early in January it was reported that an RAF raid had hit Hitler's Chancellery in Berlin. Later in the month Bomber Command continued the onslaught against the city, which had started in 1943. Six hundred Lancasters and Halifaxes dropped over 2,300 tons of bombs in a little over thirty minutes. In just two months more than 17,000 tons of bombs fell on Berlin.

What was known as Operation Steinbock took place between January and May 1944. This was a nighttime strategic bombing

Nurses in uniform. (With thanks to Brenda Sowerby)

campaign against London and southern England and was the last of its kind by the Luftwaffe. Göring believed that this offensive would dissuade the Allies from their continued assaults on German cities. The main aim of the offensive was to attack Greater London and the surrounding area, which very much affected Essex. The operation became known as the 'Baby Blitz'. Many of the bombs were incendiaries, resulting in a large number of fires. Although the Germans lost 309 aircraft during the operation they gained very little, apart from instilling fear into the civilians subjected to the drone of planes overhead by night. However, their bomber force was seriously reduced by the losses of both men and aircraft and this meant that they were not available later during the Normandy landings. This was the last large-scale manned bombing of Britain during the war. Over the five months of the operation 1,556 civilians were killed and 2,916 injured.

At the beginning of January, Sir Edwin Lutyens died. He had been responsible for many architectural works. The Cenotaph in Whitehall and many other war memorials, including one in Southend-on-Sea, were his designs. His work was also to be found in the many war cemeteries in France, Belgium and England. The simplicity of many of his works was what made them so impressive.

In mid-January 1944, an unexploded 50kg bomb was found on the Frinton Park Estate between Frinton and Walton. It was believed this was probably dropped on the night of 17/18 August the previous year. Since then it had lain undetected. The threat from 'friendly fire' also continued. Three properties in Frinton received minor damage caused by shrapnel from anti-aircraft guns. At the end of the month two more properties, one in Frinton and the other in Walton, were damaged in the same way, On 11 March 1944 Walton and Frinton were honoured to receive a visit from General Montgomery. This was during his tour of invasion forces in Britain.

It was on 20 August 1944 that the American Liberty ship SS *Richard Montgomery* was wrecked off the Nore sandbank, not far from Southend. On board were around 1,400 tonnes of explosives. Since that time she has lain in her final resting place, still with much of her cargo on board. She had arrived in the Thames Estuary where she came under the control of the Thames Naval Authority, based at the end of Southend Pier, and was ordered by the harbour master to anchor off Sheerness. There she would await the formation of a convoy.

This Hawker Hurricane CZH was flown by Squadron Leader J. Worrell DFC during July 1940. (With thanks to Canvey Bay Museum)

Unfortunately she dragged her anchor and ran aground on a sandbank. When the tide went down her back was broken. On 23 August a stevedore company was charged with removing the cargo. This was started, but the next day the hull cracked open and several cargo holds at the bow end flooded. Removal of the cargo continued into September but then the operation was abandoned. The ship, broken in two, has remained in its wrecked state ever since, approximately five miles from Southend. At low tide her three masts can still be seen. Explosives remain on board but it is considered too dangerous to remove them, so instead there is an exclusion zone around the wreck.

Music was important for keeping up moral in wartime. Across Essex, in factories and private homes, the latest songs rang out. During the 1914–18 War most of the songs were suitable for accompanying marching feet, but in the Second World War they were far more sentimental. 'There'll be Blue Birds over the White Cliffs of Dover' and 'A Nightingale Sang in Berkeley Square' became favourites, especially with the troops as they were a reminder of home. Gracie Fields, Vera Lynn and George Formby were very popular and Bing Crosby's interpretation of Irving Berlin's 'White Christmas' became an instant and lasting success. The arrival of the American big band sound made a great impression and tunes like 'String of Pearls' and 'In the Mood' as played by Glen Miller and the American Air Force Band remain popular today.

At RAF Hornchurch, as the year started, many of the planes were used to escort the US Eighth and Ninth Air Forces' Marauders which flew from nearby bases in Essex. The number of Americans serving in Essex increased dramatically. At the outbreak of war the county had just five military airfields, but by early in 1944 the number had grown to twenty-three. Of these, men of the USAAF were to be found at sixteen. At one point there were 45,000 US airmen in Essex and 15,000 from the Royal Air Force.

By this time it was realized that before long there would be a return to the Continent. Hornchurch was ready, but then the blow fell. There were seven Sector airfields but on 18 February 1944 the Sector Control Room at Hornchurch was closed down. Over the years of war the airfield had a proud record of highly successful operations. Although the Sector Room was closed the Hornchurch Squadrons continued to function, but they were now under the control of North Weald Sector. In April 80, 229 and 274 Squadrons brought their Spitfires back from Italy to be refitted and reorganized. They left on 18 May, the last Spitfire squadrons to use the airfield. This was the end of the airfield's time as an active fighter base although it remained as an RAF station.

The Allies continued to make advances in Europe and beyond and the government was busy planning for the time after victory was declared. The creation of a national health service was being discussed by the Coalition Cabinet. An Education Bill was to be introduced to raise the school leaving age, at first to fifteen and later to sixteen.

In early January news broke that a new fighter aircraft had been developed. Few details were given, but it would not need a propeller and instead would be propelled by a jet engine. The inspiration behind this development was Group Captain Frank Whittle. The plane was known as the Gloster Meteor. By February the Americans were having successes in the Pacific Islands against the Japanese and the Soviets made progress against the German army. Monte Cassino, a Benedictine

A reconstructed plotting table. (With thanks to the Norfolk RAF Air Defence Radar Museum)

monastery in Italy, had been occupied by the Germans as a defensive position blocking the Allied advance on Rome. Some felt that the destruction of this religious house could not be justified. However, the government insisted that the building was of far less importance than the Allied lives being lost.

Essex is a very diverse county. There are coastal areas and holiday towns, agricultural regions, large towns and small villages. When the war started the boundaries of the county were different from those we see today. In 1965 East Ham and West Ham county boroughs and the districts of Barking and Dagenham, Hornchurch, Ilford, Leyton, Romford, Walthamstow, Wanstead and Woodford became the London boroughs of Barking and Dagenham, Havering, Newham, Redbridge and Waltham Forest. In this book they are treated as part of Essex, as they were throughout the war. It is therefore apparent how close some parts of the county were to London and the devastating bombing that took place there.

Joan Green, née Garrod, was born in 1936 and has vivid memories of growing up in Barking during the war. She lived in Clarkson Road. One of the treats of her childhood years was being taken to the pie and mash shop and then to the cinema, known locally as 'The Bug Hole'! On one occasion, while they were there, the siren went off and everyone set out for the main public shelter. That was when they heard the approach of an enemy plane. Without hesitation the mothers pushed their children to the ground and lay over them as protection. There was the sound of machine-gun fire but, miraculously, no one was hurt.

When they were at home, if the siren went, they hurried to the Anderson shelter in the garden. This became a home for mice and spiders so it was not a popular place to stay for any length of time. Joan's older brother Roy loved school and refused to go out to the shelter until he was dressed in his full school uniform, including his shoes, socks and tie. Mrs Garrod was on her own at this time as her husband was serving with the Navy. She decided, rather than allowing her son to become distressed, she would clear out the cupboard under the stairs and put a mattress inside. Many Barking houses had been bombed, but it was noticed that nearly always the stairs and supporting wall survived so it was felt that the family would be reasonably safe there. On another occasion Joan's Uncle Ben and his family were in

Soldiers at Warley Barracks. (With thanks to Sylvia Kent)

Joan Garrod with her brother Roy. (With thanks to Joan Green)

their Anderson shelter during a raid when he decided he needed some cigarettes. His wife told him to wait until the raid was over, but he refused and set out for the shop. That was when a bomb fell and the unfortunate man lost his life.

For a while Mr Garrod's ship was in Scotland and the family set off to be nearby. Their mother probably felt that this would be safer than living so close to London. The children went to school, but they were not well received by the other pupils. They were expected to sing 'There'll Always be a Scotland while England is Below'. Joan refused and ended up in trouble. Her brother tried to persuade her to sing, without success. The other children even cut her hair, but in time they became friendly. Eventually the family left Scotland and the other pupils from the school came to see them off. Joan pulled down the sash cord window, put out her head and sang 'There'll Always Be an England'. However, everyone waved as the train left the station. Once back in Barking both children returned to their old school which Roy loved and Joan hated. Whenever the siren went she ran home to be with her mother as she was alone in the house. Needless to say the teachers soon stopped that from happening. Joan feels that the war completely disrupted her education, something that has affected her throughout her life.

February 1944 saw the lifting of clothing restrictions. Turn-ups, double-breasted jackets and lined pockets were once more allowed. Women could have pleated skirts and more buttons, but rationing continued. Austerity clothing needed fewer coupons than unrestricted garments.

In March it was announced that an Allied force had landed in Burma by glider 200 miles behind the Japanese lines. Within just twelve hours an airstrip had been carved out of the jungle capable of taking a fighter squadron. This operation was carried out by both British and American forces, each playing a vital part.

By late April plans were well under way for an Allied invasion of Europe. Overseas travel by diplomats based in London was banned as were visits to the coast. Southern England was used for military exercises, but fake troop concentrations and dummy ships were used to confuse the enemy. All preparations were kept as secret as possible.

It was also in April that the first of a planned 500,000 prefabricated homes went on show in London. They were of single- storey design

John Garrod's medals. (With thanks to Joan Green)

for bombed-out families and servicemen after demobilization. Many were eventually erected in Essex, as a large number of homes had been destroyed close to the county border. They covered 616 square feet, and had a living room, two bedrooms, a bathroom, lavatory and kitchen. This was equipped with a washing copper, cooking stove, sink and refrigerator. There was also a space-saving kitchen table that could fold flat against the wall. Made by the motor industry, these homes could be constructed in just a few hours. Their small gardens were often beautifully maintained by the proud new residents.

In the spring the Red Army continued to make progress. April saw the Germans being swept out of the Crimea and by May the Soviets had regained control of the entire region. Also in May British and Polish troops finally took the ruins of Monte Cassino, opening the way to the north of Italy.

It was early in June that the long-awaited invasion of Europe by the Allies finally began. This became known as D-Day. In the days leading up to the invasion many Essex towns saw large convoys of military vehicles filling their streets. Some had been waiting to move in parks and other open spaces. In Brentwood two of the large parks surrounding old mansions were used to gather troops and equipment ready for the journey to Normandy. These were at Weald Park and Thorndon Hall Park. Deer had roamed the grounds at Weald, but some escaped when the fences were broken. Their descendants are still free. One carriageway of the Southend Arterial Road, now better known as the A127, was closed and turned into a giant vehicle park ready for the move to the coast and then to Europe and the planned invasion. Girls at Brentwood County High School were well aware that something unusual was happening as the transport continued to roll by throughout the day. Pupils who went home to lunch on 6 June returned with the news that the Allied forces had landed on the Normandy beaches early in the morning. Surely the end of the war could not be too far away.

The evening before D-Day airfields in south-east England had seen planes taking off filled with parachutists, ready to land behind the enemy lines. Gliders too were used. Throughout the night RAF bombers pounded the German batteries along the French coast. Then, at daybreak, the US Eighth Air Force took over with their heavy bombers, escorted by Mustangs, Lightnings and Thunderbolts. Meanwhile the Royal Navy took on the dangerous task of sweeping enemy mines from the planned invasion route.

A massive invasion fleet arrived, drawn from many British ports. Battleships moored out at sea and destroyers closer inshore pounded the coastal defences. Engineers demolished obstacles on the beaches while troops and tanks came up behind them. It appears that the Germans believed the main attack would come from further along the coast and they concentrated their main force in the Pas de Calais. The names of the landing sites have become well known since the original invasion: Utah and Omaha for the Americans, Gold, Juno and Sword for the British and Canadians.

The Allies moved inland. The Germans resisted but they were finally defeated. However, the number of reported casualties was high. The British had 1,842 killed and many missing or wounded. Of the Americans 3,082 were killed, 13,121 wounded and 7,959 missing. Canadian casualties consisted of 363 killed, 1,359 wounded and 1,093 missing.

John Garrod's cartoon. (With thanks to Joan Green)

Many Essex men were involved, one of whom was Denis Self, a nineteen-year-old from Foulness Island. He landed on Juno Beach at 0900 hours on the third day of the landings. He was a driver, but water caused his engine to stall. He stayed with his vehicle by the roadside and came under fire from the enemy in a nearby water tower. Because of security surrounding the D-Day landings his family had no idea of his whereabouts. They finally received news that he was safe and well when the vicar of the local church arrived with a letter. Denis survived the war, married and settled on Foulness in the village of Church End. Another Foulness man, Henry Hump, was also involved in the D-Day invasion. He joined the army in 1943 and was posted to the Royal Engineers and trained in all forms of field work, including minelaying and the driving of all types of field equipment, including cranes and bulldozers. He arrived in France in 1944 as a fully trained Sapper and served in a special emergency detachment of twelve men. They were ready to respond to any call for help at any time or place. Later he served in France, Belgium, Holland and Germany. He was in Hamburg when the war ended and there he stayed until his demob in June 1946.

The ordinary citizens of Britain had little time to enjoy the news of success in Europe. On 13 June the first of a new type of menace was launched by the Germans. This was Hitler's promised 'secret weapon'. Officially called the V-1 flying bomb it was better known as the 'Buzz Bomb' because it made an intermittent buzzing sound. The Americans named it the doodlebug. To the Germans it was Vergeltungswaffe 1 which meant 'Revenge Weapon 1'. German cities, especially Berlin, had been devastated by non-stop Allied bombing and this was to be Hitler's revenge. It was an early unmanned pulse jet-powered cruise missile. The plan was to launch them in a terror campaign against London. On the first day a church, a convent, a hospital and a house were destroyed. In the following months these strange weapons brought fear to the whole of south-east England. Their operational range was 160 miles (250km). They flew trailing a tail of flame behind them, so many people at first thought they were enemy planes on fire. Later those who heard them said that the most terrifying time was when the engine stopped. Then there would be a few seconds of complete silence before the bomb fell to earth with approximately one ton of explosives on board. In that time of silence no one could be sure where

A minefield control tower at Coalhouse Fort. (F.J. Clamp)

it would come down and who would be the next victim. By 18 June 500 V-1 flying bombs had been fired, many of these falling on the eastern outskirts of London.

It was in July 1944 that Alan Parrish and his family had their most terrifying experience of the war. They were all in one room and were awakened around midnight by the spluttering sound of a Doodlebug, flying low and seeming to be going round in circles. They lay petrified in their beds, unable to reach the comparative safety of the Anderson shelter, or even the table. Then the engine stopped. The following explosion shook the house, blew out the windows and also the front door. Their beds were covered in broken glass and splinters of wood. The V-I had fallen about 100 yards from Alan's home, destroying two houses and both of the families caught inside.

At this point, to counter the effect of the threat, around 800 anti-aircraft guns were relocated to the coast. It was believed that the guns would have a better chance of success away from built-up areas. A thousand barrage balloons were also raised to stop the advancing weapons. Fighter pilots also became involved, especially those flying Spitfires. They undertook the dangerous operation of matching their speed to that of the flying bomb, getting in close and then tipping over its wings, thus upsetting the course of the weapon. This operation was best carried out over water as the warheads could still explode. If they were attacked over land this could cause devastation. More guns and barrage balloons were hastily put in place, but many of the V-1s still managed to get through. Any optimism that the threat would soon pass was short-lived. Before the end of the year Germany launched an even deadlier weapon.

The flying bombs were mostly fired from the Pas-de-Calais on the northern French coast and from coastal sites in Holland. Many of these passed over Essex. The first to be seen over Walton was reported on 16 June and heading towards Harwich. After that, throughout June and July, a number were spotted, several crashing into the sea. The first doodlebug that fell in Brentwood was in Hill Road, soon after the earliest one was launched. Keith Hall used to visit his grandfather who had a nursery garden in Rayleigh. He travelled from Southend on the brown City Bus and more than once heard a doodlebug flying overhead. When the engine cut out he counted to ten, waiting for the explosion. There were a number of greenhouses at the nursery, heated

Coalhouse Fort across the moat. (F.J. Clamp)

by large boilers which had stoke holes. When the fires were out the stoke holes were used as shelters. On one occasion the nursery was hit by a land mine.

The late John Horsley lived in Southchurch as a child. One of his earliest memories was of his mother telling him that a doodlebug was coming. John ran from the front to the back of the house to see the flying bomb because he knew that there was a story that if you kept moving the doodlebug would miss you! Usually he and his mother hid in their Morrison shelter during raids.

Once again children, often with their mothers, left London and were evacuated, some to the same homes they had been sent to earlier. Most went to the country. This must have been unsettling, but with the capital city once again under pressure, it was thought to be the best option. In early July over one million mothers and children were relocated. Anti-aircraft guns were ineffective at first, although RAF pilots were trying to find new ways of countering this high-speed menace. It was decided that there would be no announcements concerning the locations hit by the V-1s as this would tell the enemy how far the weapons were travelling and whether adjustments were necessary. On a more positive note the Allies were busy locating and destroying the launch sites of the weapons. In the Far East the Americans were still having successes

A Spitfire Mk BL681 FN-E. (With thanks to North Weald Airfield Museum)

against the Japanese and there were Allied victories in Normandy by late July. Minsk, the last major German stronghold on Russian soil, fell to the forces of the USSR.

At home the government was still publishing encouraging news for the homeless British. They unveiled a plan to make new rentable houses available at a cost of 13/6d per week. There were to be between three and four million new homes built in the first decade after the end of the war. They would have three bedrooms, a well-equipped kitchen and improved heating arrangements with constant hot water. This certainly showed great optimism when so many properties were still being destroyed. At the peak of the doodlebug onslaught more than 100 were fired in one day towards south-east England.

By August there was jubilation in Paris with the removal of the Nazi Swastika from the Eiffel Tower. After four appalling years the Tricolour was once again seen flying in the city. However, late in the month the Maidenek concentration camp in Poland was revealed to the press. It was estimated that 1.5 million people of all nations and creeds were murdered in the camp. There had been previous rumours concerning the horrors of these camps but this was the first real proof.

As Essex, London and the south-eastern counties still struggled to come to terms with the effects of the V-1s it was announced in Germany that the V-2 rocket was ready for launching. This was the first long-range ballistic missile in the world. It was described as being silent, except for a tearing sound, and was the first man-made object

A model of a wartime police officer. (With thanks to North Weald Airfield Museum)

to cross the boundary of space. The forerunner of these deadly weapons reached Chiswick in West London in September, killing three, Mrs Ada Harrison, three-year-old Rosemary Clarke and Sapper Bernard Browning. The latter was unfortunate enough to be on leave from the Royal Engineers at the time. Another rocket landed in Essex at Epping, but there were no casualties. The weapons weighed fifteen tons and carried one-ton warheads. It was claimed that the blast wave, caused when the weapon hit the ground, could be felt several miles away. At first the arrival of these new weapons was kept secret from the civilian population. The frequent explosions were reported as problems at gas works. It was not until 10 November that Winston Churchill finally informed Parliament about the rocket attacks. The V-2 attacks resulted in many deaths and injuries. It has been claimed that 9,000 civilians and military personal were killed and as many as 12,000 forced labourers and concentration camp prisoners died as they were forced to produce the weapons.

There has been a huge tower dominating the cliff top at Walton-on-the-Naze since 1720–1. Built by Trinity House it originally had a beacon on the top to guide shipping. It was topped by crenellations, but these were removed towards the end of the war when a massive radar dish was installed. There were billets for RAF personnel nearby and barbed wire surrounded the site. 1944 saw the establishment of one of the first guided missile test sites in the country at Walton. Further along the Naze there were anti-aircraft rocket launchers and a battery of 3.7in anti-aircraft guns. These pointed seawards, ready to bring down any V-1 flying bombs travelling over the coast on their way inland.

In early August there were reports that some German troops were leaving the Channel Islands, the only British soil they had occupied. The people of the islands were close to starvation and meat had become completely unobtainable. By September there were more successes reported in Europe. Allied troops continued to report gains in France, Belgium, Holland and Luxemburg. Sweden said it would deny entry to any Germans attempting to flee from the advancing forces. As the enemy retreated from Holland and Belgium dykes were breached in an attempt to slow down the Allied advance.

On 17 September 1944 Operation Market-Garden was launched by the Allies in Holland. Airborne troops were dropped with the intention

Vehicles ready to be transported from Fords' of Dagenham. (With thanks to The Ford Motor Company)

of securing key bridges and towns. Things did not work out as planned. There was resistance from the 9th and 10th SS Panzer Divisions and the battle of Arnhem followed. This lasted from 17–26 September. After nine days of fierce fighting what was left of the airborne forces was withdrawn. At this stage of the war this was a rare setback for the Allies.

This was when Acting Captain the Reverend Selwyn Thorne enters the story. Born in Southend-on-Sea in 1914 he was the son of a solicitor. Following his ordination by the Bishop of Chelmsford and serving as a curate at Woodford Green and Becton he volunteered to be a military chaplain. During Operation Market-Garden he arrived by glider, landing in a potato field. He helped to set up a first-aid post in a Calvinist parsonage. There was a hospital two miles away in Arnhem, but some of the wounded were too seriously injured to be moved. The

The remains of a V2 rocket engine. (With thanks to The Royal Gunpowder Museum)

chaplain stayed with them, giving help and comfort wherever he could. When the retreat was ordered a week later little food remained and there were no longer any medical supplies, but he stayed with the patients until they could finally be moved to Arnhem. He survived the war and converted to Roman Catholicism, finally dying in August 2015 aged 101.

Much to the relief of the majority of the civilian population, black-out restrictions were lifted in September. Unfortunately many coastal areas remained in darkness. Although attacks by manned aircraft were now rare, there could still be attacks from the sea, so Essex, with its long coastline, continued to be in darkness at night in many places.

By October, as Essex residents began to hope that at least some of the war-time restrictions might be coming to an end, it was announced in Germany that food rations were to be reduced. The weekly bread allowance was cut by 200g (3oz) to 2.2kg (1lb). As the Allies had

A model of a pilot in uniform. (With thanks to North Weald Airfield Museum)

further successes in Europe life in Germany became ever more difficult although attacks continued at home. Many V-1 bases were destroyed, but the V-2s presented more problems as they could be launched from mobile pads.

Between 16 and 18 October several V-1s came down and caused damage in the area around Walton. The first of these landed close to the Walton-Kirby road and left a crater of ten by twenty feet. Ninety houses were damaged, although there were no serious casualties. The next day a flying bomb was brought down by anti-aircraft guns at Lower Kirby. Again there was some localized damage to property, but no casualties. On the third night a V-1 impacted in Frinton causing considerable damage. Three houses were destroyed and twenty-three others nearby were badly damaged. There was further damage caused by anti-aircraft shrapnel. Fortunately only two minor casualties were reported. On 17 November there was an explosion at sea off Walton and Frinton. This was thought to have been caused by a V-2. V-1s continued to be seen in the area, some exploding close by.

By October 1944 Hitler realized that an Allied invasion of Germany was imminent. He issued an order for all able-bodied males to be called up for a newly-formed force, the Volkssturm or People's Guard. The headquarters were to be in the mountain caves of Salzkammergut in Bulgaria. In spite of this late attempt to stop the invasion of Germany the first city, Aachen, fell to the Allies at the end of the month. As the Volkssturm was coming into being the threat of the invasion of Britain had disappeared and the Home Guard finally stood down towards the end of the year. In Essex the Home Guard had been constantly ready to defend the coastline, airfields, factories and ammunition stores from possible attack. At its peak there had been 1,084 battalions throughout the country, with 1,701,208 men and 31,824 women.

As the year drew to a close fighting continued in Europe, but the government continued to make plans for a victorious future. In December it was announced that express highways would be built once peace was restored. New towns would come into being as so many people had lost their homes during the Blitz. There was to be a green belt around the city, limiting any further London sprawl. A ring road around the capital was also to be considered. Would the New Year bring the longed-for victory? The government was obviously optimistic, but time alone would tell.

General Montgomery visiting The Ford Motor Company at Dagenham. (With thanks to The Ford Motor Company)

To
The Ford Motor Coy
Dagenham

Understand you are busily engaged in producing spare parts for all types of vehicles. I am delighted to hear this news. A plentiful supply of spare parts is vital to the success of any operation in the field.

B. L. Montgomery
General
C-in-C 21 Army Group

22-2-44

A letter from General Montgomery. (With thanks to The Ford Motor Company)

CHAPTER SEVEN

1945

Victory

1945 was possibly the most important year of the twentieth century, but war still raged as January dawned and new horrors were discovered. At the end of the month Auschwitz fell into Soviet hands. Here Jews from all over Europe had been sent to the gas chambers or made to work under horrendous conditions. By that time the majority of the surviving inmates had been removed to Germany. Of the 5,000 still at the camp all were close to death from starvation and disease. Mounds of skeletal corpses were also discovered, unburied and left to rot.

In Essex Christmas had been celebrated with a little more cheer than in recent years, but there was still the fear of sudden V2 attacks. Many children's toys were of cardboard or home-made, but were still greatly appreciated and an effort was made to decorate homes.

In the Far East the Americans continued to make advances against the Japanese and the Soviets had successes against the Germans. The RAF and US Airforce were still busy attacking German cities. In mid-February a day and night of non-stop bombardment of Dresden ended with this once beautiful city being reduced to rubble. Although formerly noted for its historic buildings and fine artwork it was also an industrial centre and an important centre of communications for the German armies on the Eastern Front. No completely accurate statistics could be given for the numbers killed, but it ran to many thousands and there was considerable criticism of the operation at home.

In the north-east of Essex there were still frequent reports of flying bombs approaching the area. One came to earth in fields not far from Great Holland Church on 13 January. Fortunately on this occasion there were no casualties or damage to buildings. The V-1s were terrifying,

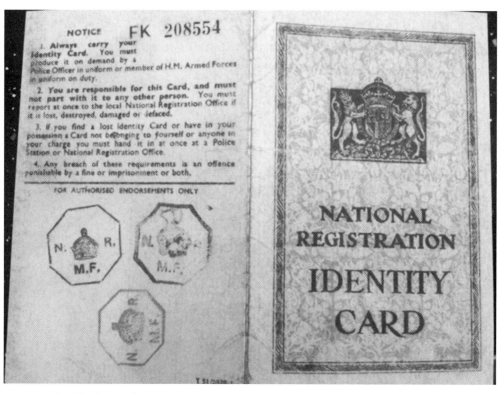

An identity card.

but there was a good chance that these could be destroyed by fighter aircraft or anti-aircraft fire before doing more damage further into Essex and London. The V-2 was a different matter entirely. It was a ballistic missile that descended from a high altitude and there was no real defence. Two of these were believed to have come down over the sea near Frinton and Walton early in February. Some buildings were damaged by a V-2 on 10 February and another attack two days caused minor damage to property. A V-2 rocket fell close to the railway in Kirby on the 17th of the month. Again some properties were damaged. Two more of the rockets came down before the end of the month, one being in the Clacton area.

In February the leaders of Great Britain, the United States of America and the Soviet Union met at Yalta in the Crimea. The decisions made by these three men, Winston Churchill, Roosevelt and Stalin would have far reaching effects on the future throughout the world when Germany was finally defeated. Agreement was reached on how the country would be divided and what penalties would follow. Plans were also made for the invasion of mainland Japan.

Thursday 29 March was important for the Frinton and Walton Urban District as this was the day of the last incident to affect the inhabitants. Early in the morning a V-1 was brought down in fields close to Great Holland by anti-aircraft fire. The weapon had been packed with small incendiary bombs which would have caused considerable damage if it had been able to fly further. There was some minor damage to local properties caused by the anti-aircraft fire.

In March more German cities fell to the advancing Allies. There were also successes in the Far East. The centre of Tokyo was bombarded with fire bombs and later in the month all schools and universities in the city were closed as everyone over the age of six was ordered to do war work. In Britain former Prime Minister David Lloyd George died aged eighty-two. He had been the Liberal Prime Minister from 1916 to 1922 and is remembered as an outstanding orator.

The 1st Battalion, The Essex Regiment, which was part of the Regular Army, served in Sudan, Egypt, Libya, Syria and Burma. It also operated in support as the battles of Imphal and Kohima were fought against the Japanese. These two battles were of great importance as they helped to turn the war against Japan in the Far East.

The 2nd Battalion of the Essex Regiment was with the BEF in France in 1940. The troops were evacuated from the beaches of Dunkirk during the Battle of France. On D-Day in June 1944 they were part of the force landing on Gold Beach. The Battalion took part in the Battle of Le Havre and also fought in the battle for Caen. Towards the end of the war the men were with the First Canadian Army. In 1945 they were also involved in the Second Battle of Arnhem. When the war ended the 2nd Battalion had recorded more than 800 men killed, wounded or missing.

The 7th (Home Defence) Battalion, Essex Regiment, existed for home defence operations in Britain. It first came into being in 1939 and the members were mainly older men or those who were less fit but

This organ was used throughout the war at the North Weald Chapel. (With thanks to the North Weald Airfield Museum)

A reconstruction at the Essex Regimental Museum, with thanks.

had former military experience. There were also some younger men aged between eighteen and nineteen. The 8th Battalion was raised in 1940 and stationed at Warley Barracks, close to Brentwood, as was the 9th Battalion. They were later transferred to the Royal Artillery, but they retained their Essex Regiment cap badges. The regiment took part in the Battle of Normandy as part of the 9th Army Royal Artillery.

The 50th (Holding) Battalion also came into existence in 1940, having been formed in Colchester. Later it became the 10th Battalion, serving in a home defence role, assigned to 223rd Independent Infantry Brigade (Home). Late in 1942 the Brigade became the 3rd Para Brigade and was involved in the creation of the 6th Airborne Division. This led to participation in the D-Day landings. The Battalion was involved in the destruction of the Merville Gun Battery. After that the troops fought in the Battle of Normandy in their original role as infantrymen. Throughout the war the Essex Regiment served with distinction and the part it played is remembered with great pride.

April 1945 was a momentous month as far as the Allies were concerned. In the Far East the Americans took Okinawa and their navy sank the largest battleship in the Japanese fleet, the *Yamato*. April 15th saw the liberation of the Bergen-Belsen concentration camp. Referring to these camps Winston Churchill said, 'No words can express our horror'. Nuremberg fell to the Allied forces on Adolf Hitler's fifty-sixth birthday. This had previously been the scene of some of the massive Nazi rallies where the Führer had made emotional speeches to encourage his followers.

Education throughout Essex was disrupted during the war. There are many stories that could be told, but in the book to celebrate the fiftieth anniversary of Brentwood County High School there is an excellent record of the effect the V-1 and V-2 attacks had on the school during the later stages of the conflict. Shortly after the D-Day landings the first of the V-1s passed close by. Most of the School Certificate examinations had to be held in brick-built shelters that year. Pupils listened for the sound of approaching doodlebugs followed by a far more terrifying silence before the bomb crashed to earth.

On the first night of the V-1s the air-raid warning sounded and people moved into shelters Gunfire seemed to carry on all night, leading to extremely tired pupils and staff arriving the next day. An application was made to the education authority in Chelmsford to close

A party for children at Fords' of Dagenham. Many of the children still look extremely anxious. (With thanks to The Ford Motor Company)

the school for the afternoon, but this was firmly rejected with no sympathy given. Radar could predict the arrival of the missiles and the siren was sounded, so everyone was expected to take shelter. Once the weapon had passed, or come down, the all-clear was given. This frequently led to disturbed nights and constantly interrupted lessons. On one occasion the whole school had to move to the shelters thirteen times in a single day!

During the time of the Higher and School Certificate examinations it was decided that they should take place as usual in the school hall. Two members of staff were placed on duty outside the front door. When they heard the drone of an approaching V-1 one would hurry to the hall and blow a whistle. At that point the pupils were expected to rise in complete silence and move to the brick shelters situated beside the entrance hall. There they waited, still in silence, until a staff member, having heard the 'all-clear', led them back to their papers in the hall. Once, the staff member responsible for blowing the whistle, accidentally put her finger over the hole and no sound could be heard. However, the students realized her intention, rose and moved in silence to the shelters. During the war everyone did their best to obey the rules and keep safe.

Sadly it was reported that President Roosevelt had died on the 12 April. He had been a great Democratic politician and had served as President four times. Ill health had dogged him for a number of years, but he had never let it stop him. Unfortunately he did not live long enough to see the end of the Second World War. The Vice-President, Harry S. Truman, was sworn in as the thirty-second President of the United States of America.

From Italy news came that Mussolini had been found by partisans hiding under a pile of coats whilst travelling in a convoy of eight cars. After a brief trial he and those with him were condemned to death and shot. His mistress, Clara Petacci was also killed. They were then strung up by their feet outside a petrol station in Milan's Piazza Loretto. The next day the last men still fighting against the Allies in Italy surrendered to Field Marshal Alexander, the Allied Commander.

On the final day of the month news broke of the death of Hitler in a Berlin bunker. He was found by members of his staff lying on a sofa with a gunshot wound through his mouth. A pistol lay on the floor next to him. Beside him was the body of Eva Braun, dead from poison. They had married the previous day. Almost to the very end he still appeared to believe that his armies would triumph.

Frank Dudley, a former Lancaster bomber navigator and later a professional footballer. (F.J. Clamp)

Winston Churchill had once described him as a 'bloodthirsty guttersnipe'.

Back in Great Britain there was a new feeling of optimism. Radios brought daily news of what was happening in Europe and beyond. When the announcement came that Adolf Hitler was dead there was disbelief and then jubilation. Surely, with their leader gone, the Germans would be unable to continue the war for long. Victory was in the air. The last V-2 rocket in Brentwood had fallen in Hutton Park in March 1945. As the Allies advanced further attacks grew increasingly unlikely.

By the end of April 120,000 German troops had been captured by the Allied forces during the final campaign in Italy. As a growing number of Nazi concentration camps were discovered it was estimated that eleven million had died in these horrendous prisons. The majority were Jews, but there were also Slavs, homosexuals, Roma people, the disabled and those who were considered enemies of the Nazi regime. As news of the horrors endured in the camps broke many found it almost impossible to believe that one group of humans could have inflicted such horror and degradation on another.

As May arrived it became obvious to every British citizen that the end of the war was imminent. Not that everyone in Germany shared this view. Grand Admiral Karl Dönitz had been chosen by Hitler to succeed him as Führer. The new leader had been captured towards the end of the Great War and had spent a year in Manchester Lunatic Asylum – perhaps not the leader most people would have chosen. However, on 1 May he declared himself to be Hitler's successor. Yet, by the following day, 1,000,000 German troops had surrendered in Italy and Austria. The Germans also surrendered in Holland and Denmark and on 5 May the same thing happened in Norway.

May 7th saw the final surrender of Germany. This happened at 2.41 am in Rheims. The location was a tiny schoolhouse where General Eisenhower had his headquarters. General Alfred Jodl, Army Chief of Staff and the German emissary, signed the instrument of unconditional surrender. On behalf of the Western Allies General Bedell Smith, Chief of Staff to General Eisenhower, signed and General Ivan Suslapatov acted as the witness for the Soviet Union. Just three days before, to the south of Hamburg on Luneburg Heath, Field Marshal Montgomery had already received the surrender of all the German forces in North West Germany, Holland and Denmark. This happened in Montgomery's tent. May 8th was announced as Victory in Europe Day, although the Soviet Union and some other Eastern European countries chose 9 May to be their Victory Day.

At the end of the First World War hostilities ceased on one day. In the Second World War, with fighting having taken place on so many fronts, the timetable was different. In the Far East Japan was not ready

The former Officers' Mess at Warley. This is now the Marillac Hospital. (F.J. Clamp)

to surrender. As many families prepared to welcome home members who had been involved in the European conflict, others realized that they would need to wait longer and hope that their loved ones would eventually return.

Many people heard the news on their radios. Pamela and Frances Winn were in their bedroom in Prittlewell when their mother came in carrying a flag. This was how the children discovered that the war in Europe was over. It was time for the celebrations to begin. The flag was then hung outside the window. Very soon other houses were bedecked with flags and bunting. The girls were given red, white and blue ribbons for their hair, obviously bought some time earlier, ready for this momentous day.

Alma Sproggs walked to Southend from Westcliff on VE Day. People were dancing, singing and kissing each other in the high street, outside the Odeon cinema, and she joined in. Being a seaside town it was possible to hear ships sirens sounding over the water as those on board enjoyed their own celebrations.

Maureen Ollett, née Powl, lived at 38 Capel Gardens, Ilford with her parents, Archie and Elsie and sister Eileen. During the years of war Maureen remembers a bomb passing through the top floor of Number

47, crossing the road and landing on Number 54. The occupants of Number 47 were unhurt but a young girl at Number 54 was killed. Other houses were severely damaged at this time and were demolished later. Maureen vividly recalls two street parties held in her road, one for VE Day and a later one for Victory in Japan Day. In 2010 some of those who had lived in Capel Gardens during the momentous years of the war returned for a reunion where memories of wartime childhood were once again relived.

Alan Parrish also has clear memories of VE Day. Normally reserved adults raced into the street, jumped up and down, hugged each other and even burst into song, especially singing the songs made popular during the war. As Alan says, 'The elation was spontaneous and very un-British, but a testament to the joy felt by the nation.'

As the news broke of the end of the war many people rushed to London to join in the celebrations and to reach Buckingham Palace in the hope of seeing the Royal Family on the balcony. King George VI, Queen Elizabeth and the two princesses duly appeared to rapturous cheers and applause from those waiting below. The centre of the city became the venue for a giant street party. The years of austerity were

A house in Ilford decorated to celebrate victory. (With thanks to Maureen Ollett)

still far from being over, but this was a chance to enjoy a few moments of celebration. Bomb damage was all too evident, but on that day it could be ignored. Locally women began thinking about street parties for the children and every road began to make plans. Some of these did not come to fruition for several months. Rationing was still in force, but many had small stores of treats that could be used to make a party memorable. Pamela, Frances and Clive Winn all went to a party in Beedell Avenue, Westcliff. The road is on a hill and slopes down to Fairfax Drive, but trestle tables were erected and no-one seemed to have problems with the gradient. Lois Holmes, née Hance, lived in Flemming Crescent in Leigh on Sea. At that time the road was unsuitable for a party so it was agreed that the children could join the celebration in Woodleigh Avenue. Many bonfires were lit and Lois attended one on land in Rayleigh Drive. This was topped with a large effigy of Adolf Hitler. As far as possible all the children wore red, white and blue. Bunting and flags were everywhere and shop windows were also decorated in red, white and blue.

Adults too had a chance to celebrate. The Kursaal Pleasure Ground was open and Elvina Savill remembered going there on VE Day. There were dances and she attended one with two soldiers who had taken part in the D-Day landings. They had been slightly wounded and been sent to Southend for Rest and Recuperation. The Kursaal had always been a centre for dances as it had an excellent ballroom. This was used for some of the celebrations. The soldiers from the garrison at Shoebury put on a special show for local people. This was to thank them for the support they had given throughout the war and it went on for three days with dances in the evening, the music being played by military bands. Colchester saw fireworks, bonfires and even searchlight displays.

Although the war in the Far East continued Britain prepared to enter a new stage politically. There had been no general election since 1935. A coalition government had been in charge throughout the war, led by Winston Churchill since May 1940. In late May he resigned, but was asked by the King to form a caretaker government. This was agreed, although arrangements were made for Parliamentary elections on 5 July. Party politics could once more return. A Royal Proclamation finally dissolved Parliament on 15 June. In the same month the division of Germany was agreed, with the European Advisory Council defining

The apse end of the Royal Anglian Regiment and the Essex Regiment Chapel at Warley. (F.J. Clamp)

future zones of occupation. On 26 June the World Security Charter was signed establishing an international peacekeeping organization to be known as the United Nations.

Essex was slowly returning to some sort of normality as election fever began to grip the county. Some felt great loyalty to Winston Churchill, their wartime leader. Others believed that it was time for change. In the end it was the Labour Party that gained a landslide victory with 393 seats to the Tories' 213. The Liberals won just twelve and Independents twenty-two. Clement Atlee became the new Prime Minister, a very different man from his predecessor. He took over a massive task as he attempted to rebuild a country exhausted by war. The Labour Party manifesto had proposed a programme of public ownership and social reform. Herbert Morrison had led the party to victory and became the second man in the new government with responsibility on the Home Front. The policy changes would affect everyone throughout the country.

Housing was a major problem, especially in those areas that had suffered major bombing. In July the government gave local authorities the power to requisition empty houses. Prefabricated housing became popular, although demand greatly exceeded supply. Because of its closeness to London small estates of 'prefabs' were built throughout Essex. In Southend some even had a second floor. Requisitioning of properties could obviously cause problems when owners returned, possibly from evacuation. Many of the Plotland properties in the Basildon area were still in use. For those who had been bombed out of their London homes, these had become their permanent dwellings. They might be without mains drainage, gas, electricity, a water supply or made-up roads but the inhabitants were proud to be homeowners. In the immediate post-war period no one foresaw the changes that were yet to come.

In *Memories of Basildon* by Jim Reeves, the author recorded some of the recollections of those who had lived through the conflict. Many recalled going to school with gas masks carried in small boxes over their shoulders. They were essential to keep close by at all times, whether away or at home. Small children had red gas masks named after Micky Mouse, but often they dreaded having to wear them. In 2015, when Pamela Livingston, née Winn, was ill in hospital she was given an oxygen mask, which she kept pulling off. At first no one

The back of 'The Haven', a surviving Plotland cottage. (F.J. Clamp)

realized why, but then it was discovered that she associated this mask with the one she had been made to wear as a child.

Churchill said that Essex was one of the most heavily-bombed counties in the country. Some of the bombs fell on the little Plotland homes, often used by their owners to escape the devastation in the East End of London. Frequently other family members and former neighbours arrived at the bungalows needing a place of refuge after a particularly bad raid. Space was tight, but somewhere was always found for those in trouble. The late Albert Lee lived in one of those bungalows. On one occasion his father was about to leave the family and go back to London when Albert rushed indoors. He had just discovered a strange-looking hole about sixteen feet from their home. Mr Lee came out to look and realized that this was a bomb crater. The police were called and then an officer from the Royal Engineers arrived. The tension could be felt as he carefully removed the detonator before the offending bomb could be taken away.

Children who went to Markham Chase School in Basildon always remembered the smell in the playground shelters. A bucket was placed at one end with a curtain draped around. This was a make-shift toilet. Those who arrived first in the shelter tried to sit as far from the curtain as possible. If the raid was a long one it was even more desirable to claim a place well away from the bucket.

The demolition of Warley Barracks. This is where The Ford Motor Company's offices now stand. (With thanks to Sylvia Kent)

At the end of July Attlee, Truman and Stalin met to discuss the future of post-war Europe. Arguments developed, with the Soviet Union disagreeing with the plans put forward by the others. No agreement was reached. Winston Churchill later described what was happening as an Iron Curtain being slammed down against the West. However, as far as most of the British were concerned, these events were happening far away and nothing was going to stop their victory euphoria.

Troops from the Essex Regiment were still involved in fighting against Japan. The Japanese seemed unwilling and unlikely to surrender, however severe their losses. Drastic action was needed. On 6 August an atomic bomb was dropped on Hiroshima. Many of those who had worked on what became known as the Manhattan Project had no idea what was being created. Both the Americans and the British had been involved in the project. The devastation caused by the bomb was hard to imagine, but when photographs emerged they had to be believed. Still the Japanese did not surrender. Three days later a second bomb was dropped, this time on Nagasaki, the shipbuilding centre on the island of Kyushu. The result was horrendous with thousands of men, women and children either killed outright or left with life-changing injuries.

By 10 August, realizing that more atomic bombs would be dropped if they did not agree to peace, the Japanese surrendered to the Allies, but they wished the emperor to remain as head of state. Negotiations started and President Truman suspended all attacks while they were taking place. Finally, on 15 August 1945 the emperor announced on radio the surrender of Japan. September 2nd saw the formal signing of the surrender aboard the battleship USS *Missouri*. The war in the Far East was officially over.

It was not until midnight that news of the total surrender of the Japanese was broadcast. Ships sirens could be heard in towns on the Essex coast and train whistles were blown announcing the final ending of all hostilities. Two days of holidays followed, bonfires were lit and fireworks set off. In many places street parties had already been prepared.

A victory bonfire for children in Leigh-on-Sea. The effigy on top is of Hitler. (With thanks to Lois Holmes)

Once again the people of Essex were ready to celebrate with street parties. Photographs taken at the time still showed very anxious looking children. They had heard the words stating that peace had returned, but for those who had spent their whole lives living with the fear of sudden attacks, it would take time to accept that they were now safe. Some street parties in Essex took place immediately, but others took longer to arrange, some not happening until 1946.

The war might have officially ended, but there were many of the military who did not immediately arrive home. Among these were some prisoners of war. In 1929 the treatment of prisoners of war had been covered by the Geneva Convention. This had been signed by Britain, Italy, Germany and the USA. The Western Allies were under orders to treat all Axis prisoners in the way laid down by the Convention. There were some who ignored the orders. One such abuse occurred after the liberation of the Dachau concentration camp. Some of the SS guards were apparently shot, although they were attempting to surrender. Most Allied prisoners were treated according to the Convention by the Germans, although some faced an extreme shortage of food. This was hardly surprising as, towards the end of the war, the civilians in Germany were facing similar problems. Soviet prisoners were not treated by the Convention rules as, according to their captors, they had not signed the Geneva Convention. It has been said that of the 5.7 million Soviet captives 3.3 million died whilst being held as prisoners.

When the war started there were just two POW camps in Britain. By the end there were more than 600 and a number of these were to be found in Essex. As the hostilities drew to a close an endless stream of prisoners arrived on British soil. Some of these were sent to Warley and Thorndon Park on the outskirts of Brentwood. Ena and Una Felton remember their father bringing home some German soldiers on Christmas Day. He had met them in the town. The Felton family and other church members welcomed and looked after them. A German pastor brought a number of the prisoners from Ockendon to Brentwood for services, where they sang with great gusto. After the war one of the former prisoners returned to the area and married a young lady from Ilford. He settled down in Essex and used to visit the twins' father from time to time. Pamela Staples remembers that Italian prisoners would wait by the gates at Thorndon Park to ask passers-by

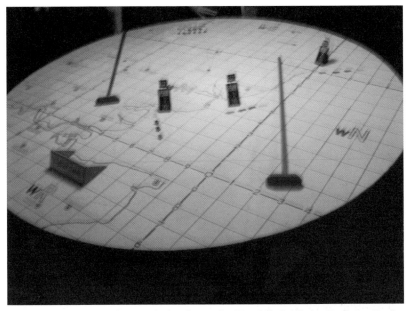

An RAF plotting table. (With thanks to the Norfolk RAF Air Defence Radar Museum)

to post their letters. She also recalls prisoners working on farms in Warley.

Most of the military did not return home as soon as the war ended. By mid-August a promise was made that the number of servicemen coming back would be increased from 115,000 per month to 171,000. Many people were also being released from their work in munitions factories. Emmanuel Shinwell, the Minister of Fuel and Power, aimed to increase coal production by 18 million tons each year.

The cost of the war, in money and human lives, was colossal. It was estimated that over 55 million had been killed, many of them civilians. It was soon realized that the rebuilding of the properties destroyed would take many years. As movement around the country became easier the number of missing houses became obvious to travellers. Close to London most roads had gaps where families had once lived. Often the stairs could still be seen and torn wallpaper showed where rooms had once been.

Well-preserved war graves at St Andrew's Church Hornchurch. The wall at the back is a simple Lutyen's design found in many War Cemeteries on the Continent. (F.J. Clamp)

By September, 1945 news was coming through of the atrocities suffered by prisoners of war in the Far East. Thousands died from disease and starvation as they worked on the railway line from Siam to Burma. There was shock as photographs emerged of the near-skeletal bodies of those who had endured appalling conditions. Manual workers were expected to toil in tropical heat whilst being given only a handful of rice each day. In October the first prisoners of war from the Far East arrived home on the liner *Corfu*, docking at Southampton. Many found it impossible to talk about the suffering they had faced in the Far East. By November the Nuremburg trials of Nazi war criminals were under way.

As Christmas approached people throughout the country made a real effort to celebrate. Rationing was still in force but children busily made paper chains to decorate their homes and schools. They also used rolls of glitter, left over from the attempts to disrupt enemy radar. Essex no longer feared sudden attack along the coast. There might still be shortages, but there was a new feeling of freedom and hope. Surely the country would soon return to the days of pre-war prosperity.

CHAPTER EIGHT

Aftermath

The war was over. Former members of the armed forces returned home and needed to adapt to civilian life. Some found this easy, but many discovered that home life had changed for ever. In pre-war times married women usually gave up work to raise their families. A large number had found new independence during the years of conflict and were unwilling to give this up when peace returned.

Rationing had existed throughout the war years and continued beyond them. Petrol rationing had first been introduced in 1939 and continued until 1950. Food rationing had started in January 1940 and restrictions were lifted gradually, starting three years after victory had been announced. It lasted until July 1954, nine years after the end of the war and fourteen years since it had first been introduced. Clothes rationing finally ended in March 1949. This led to fresh designs in clothes and especially notable was the 'New Look', with much longer and fuller skirts. The time of large supermarkets lay in the future and for the many small family shops throughout Essex and the rest of the country the freeing of all restrictions must have come as a great relief. The last commodities to come off the ration were meat and bacon.

Former military installations have served many purposes since the end of the war. Rough Tower was one of the two sea forts off the coast of Walton. At one time it was planned to use it for Radio Caroline, a pirate radio station, but no broadcasts were made. It was taken over by Roy Bates in 1965. He was educated at Lindisfarne College, Westcliff-on-Sea and served as an infantry major during the Second World War. On one occasion when he was briefly away from the fort Radio Caroline attempted to take over, but Bates returned and with his crew removed them. In 1967 Radio Caroline's crew again tried to take the tower, but were unsuccessful. September 1976 saw Rough Tower being declared the Independent Principality of Sealand. It had its own stamps and passports. On one occasion Roy Bates even fired a shot across the bows of a Trinity House ship that he believed had come too close to the fort. Bates was arrested when he visited the mainland, but it was decided by the court that Sealand was outside British jurisdiction. On 23 June 2006 a fire in a generator caused major damage to the fort.

According to an article in the *Echo* newspaper Essex people are more likely to dig up unexploded bombs than anyone else in the country. The area between Thurrock and Southend was at very high risk during the war with around fifty bombs being dropped on each 1,000 acres of land. Anywhere bordering the Thames was vulnerable because Luftwaffe pilots viewed the area as a strategic trade target. Shoeburyness Barracks and Southend pier were obvious targets, as were the oil refineries at Thurrock. The Ford factories too and the protecting anti-aircraft guns would have been high on the Luftwaffe target lists. For every ten bombs dropped it is thought one failed to explode. One reason for the V-1s and V-2s coming down over Essex rather than reaching London, was that they were made using slave labour. It is believed some workers tampered with the navigation systems, making them miss their intended targets.

In 1946 Stanstead was first used for commercial flights. Old Halifax bombers were converted for use as cargo planes. In the 1950s the Americans returned and used the airfield for jet aircraft. Their stay was brief and after that the airfield was used for various purposes. When, in 1980, an American Air Force plane was unable to land at Mildenhall it diverted instead to Stanstead. The pilot later described Stanstead as 'an inactive airport north of London'. This was still some years before it was decided to turn the old airfield into London's third airport.

The Welfare State became a reality in the years after the war ended. In 1942 William Beveridge was charged with submitting a report on changes that would be necessary once peace was restored. This report claimed that there were five main evils in society; Want, Disease, Ignorance, Squalor and Idleness. These would be addressed in future reforms. The diet followed by many during the war had already led to some improvement in health, especially for children with orange juice, cod liver oil and free milk in schools being available.

Following the post-war elections Clement Atlee's new Labour government started acting on the recommendations. In July 1948

A Battle of Britain poster. (With thanks to North Weald Airfield Museum)

Aneurin Bevan opened the Park Hospital in Manchester and this was really when the National Health Service was born. From that time on hospitals, doctors, nurses, dentists, opticians and pharmacists were to provide a free service for all. The cost would be colossal, but it was to be paid for from taxation. By 1952 a one-shilling prescription charge was introduced and there was to be a flat rate of £1 for dental treatment. However, prescription charges were again abolished in 1965 and they remained free until 1968. There have been problems over the years, but the National Health Service is still viewed with envy by many countries.

We have seen how the war disrupted the education of thousands of children. This happened for many when they were evacuated and formal teaching often only took place for half of each day. It also affected those who stayed at home, with lessons disturbed by air-raids. This meant a move into playground shelters where lessons sometimes continued to the accompaniment of exploding bombs and anti-aircraft fire. Even before hostilities ended in 1944, the Education Act, introduced by R.A. Butler, made significant changes to the way in which children would be taught in the future. Free education must be available for all and a tripartite system was introduced for secondary schools; grammar, secondary technical and secondary modern. The leaving age was also raised to fifteen. It was intended that this should rise to sixteen as soon as possible, but this did not happen until 1972. At the age of eleven children took the 11+ examination, the result of which decided which type of education would be most suitable for each child. Every school day was required to start with a non-denominational religious activity. Essex already had a number of grammar and secondary schools, although technical schools were rarer.

The devastation caused by the bombing of many British towns and cities left the country with a major housing problem. Various solutions were tried including the construction of temporary homes and the requisitioning of empty properties. In 1946 the New Towns' Act was passed. New towns would be created to ease some of the problems. There were to be seven around London, two of them in Essex. They were often based on existing villages

Harlow was a village mentioned in the Domesday Book and is located in west Essex. In 1947 a master plan was drawn up by Sir Frederick Gibbard to develop a large New Town around the old village. It was hoped this would ease some of the overcrowding in East London. The original village would be known as Old Harlow and it would be incorporated into the new development along with Great Parndon, Latton, Tye Green, Potter Street, Churchgate Street, Little Parndon and Netteswell. It was intended that the town would be split into self-supporting neighbourhoods, each with its own shopping precinct, community facilities and a public house. Schools were also to be built to cover the full age-range of the children moving into the area. Well-known architects were invited to submit plans. The town has developed with an extensive network of cycle tracks connecting all areas to the town centre.

Another Essex New Town was Basildon, which is just thirty-two miles from London. Basildon was far from being a completely new town. It was recorded in the Domesday Book as Beorhtels Hill, although its history goes back far before that time. Four villages were incorporated into the new development; Basildon, Laindon, Pitsea and Vange. There were problems in the area. Many of the old Plotland houses needed roads built and updating to modern standards. A number had a rateable value of less than £10, so the cost of improvements would far outweigh the revenue collected. Billericay Urban District Council was responsible for making the improvements. The Council Clerk realized that, if Basildon was accepted as a New Town, all their financial problems would disappear. In spite of local opposition Basildon was designated a New Town in 1949. Soon the Plotland dwellings were demolished as Compulsory Purchase Orders were issued. It was found that were 30,000 different owners of properties in the area, many unknown or impossible to trace. The land to be considered consisted of 7,818 acres, but building went ahead. On 18 June 1951 Betty and John Walker became the first couple to receive the keys to their new home in Vange.

Like Harlow the plan was for the development of self-supporting, self-contained communities. One thing the planners did not account for was the explosion of car ownership in the post-war years and parking facilities were soon inadequate. New factories provided employment for many of those who moved into the area and once a railway station was built there was easy access to London. Parkland was also considered to be important and there are excellent recreational facilities in the town.

Great Britain is now a very different country from the one that went to war in 1939. The old bomb-damaged sites have disappeared, as have most of the installations that were erected to protect the Essex coastline. Yet the many war memorials that stand in every town and village are a constant reminder of the sacrifices made by so many in those terrifying years of conflict. Essex men and women, both at home and in the forces, bravely played their part in the war and their contribution can be remembered with pride.

8th June, 1946

To-day, as we celebrate victory, I send this personal message to you and all other boys and girls at school. For you have shared in the hardships and dangers of a total war and you have shared no less in the triumph of the Allied Nations.

I know you will always feel proud to belong to a country which was capable of such supreme effort; proud, too, of parents and elder brothers and sisters who by their courage, endurance and enterprise brought victory. May these qualities be yours as you grow up and join in the common effort to establish among the nations of the world unity and peace.

George R.I.

A letter from King George VI to schoolchildren who lived through the years of war. (With thanks to Alan Parrish)

Bibliography

Brentwood County High School 1913–1963.

Foley, Michael, *Essex. Ready for Anything*, Sutton Publishing Ltd, 2006.

Foley, Michael, *More Frontline Essex*, The History Press, 2008.

Foley Michael, *Essex at War*, Amberly Publishing, 2009.

Fryer, John, *Brentwood. A Concise Pictorial History*, Brentwood Town Centre Partnership, 2001.

Gordon, Dee, *Essex Land Girls*, The History Press, 2015.

Hussey, Stephen, *Headline History*, Essex Record Office, 2000.

Kent, Sylvia, *Brentwood Voices*, Tempus Publishing Ltd, 2001.

Kent, Sylvia, *The Billericay School*, Tempus Publishing Ltd, 2003.

Osbourne, Mike, *Defending Essex*, The History Press, 2013.

Porter, Valerie, *Yesterday's Countryside*, David & Charles, 2000.

Rayner, Geoff, *Seaside Front Line*, Foray, 2nd Edition 2005.

Smith, Eric, *First Things First*, Ian Henry Publications, 1992.

Toms, Carel, *Hitler's Fortress Islands*, The New English Library Ltd, 1967.

Acknowledgements

My thanks to all those who have given advice, shared memories and lent photographs for use in this book. So many have been involved that it is impossible to name them all individually. Special thanks are due to The Ford Motor Company, The Canvey Bay Museum, The Royal Gunpowder Mills, The North Weald Airfield Museum, The Essex Regiment Museum, The Foulness Heritage Centre and The Norfolk RAF Air Defence Radar Museum.

My thanks are also due to Sylvia and Peter Kent, Maureen Ollett, Sue Thoirs, Peter Carr, Joan Green, Helen Clamp, Brenda Sowerby, Ena Love, Una Scott and Alan Parrish. I must also mention all my family and especially my son, David, who is always ready to give technical advice. Above all my husband Roger who reads my proofs, gives advice and drives me to all the venues I need to visit.

Index